SONS OF THE FATHER

BECOMING BROTHERS WITH JESUS CHRIST

DANIEL KOOMAN

In loving memory of my Dad, Nicolaas.
Because you sought the Father and became a son,
as your son I came to know the Father.

For Mom, Chris, Andrew and Matthew. We will be family forever.

And for Judah.
You are my son, and already a true worshiper of the Father.

ENDORSEMENT FROM RABBI SCHNEIDER

Best-selling Author The Book of Revelation Decoded & Host of Discovering The Jewish Jesus

"I very much appreciate Daniel's love, passion, and fire for God. It is infectious. Daniel's deep yearning to experience more fully the reality of being the Father's son, has resulted in him being used by God to be a fountain to others.

Your identity as Father's son or daughter will be strengthened as you read Daniel's book Sons of the Father."

- Rabbi Schneider, July 2023

Sons of the Father: Becoming Brothers with Jesus Christ
Copyright © 2023 by Daniel Kooman

ISBN: 9798394038266
Independently published. All rights reserved.

No part of this publication may be reproduced, distributed or transmitted in any form or by any means, including photocopying, recording, or other electronic or mechanical methods, without prior written permission of the publisher, except in the case of brief quotations embodied in critical reviews and certain other noncommercial uses permitted by copyright law.

FIRST EDITION

To print excerpts of this book, inquire about it's contents or learn more about speaking engagements, contact:
danielkooman@unveilstudios.com

CONTENTS

SONS OF THE FATHER

Introduction 6

CH. 1: The Great Exchange of Barabbas 10

CH. 2: In A Cell With Barabbas 24

CH. 3: Sonship as a Theme in Scripture 34

CH. 4: The Last Minute Believer on the Cross 46

CH. 5: The Centurion's Declaration of Faith 56

CH. 6: 3 Women Who Helped Define Sonship 70

CH. 7: Three Rules of Sonship 104

CH. 8: Three Benefits of Sonship......................118

CH. 9: Look to the Son 140

CH. 10: Born to be Sons and Daughters 162

Epilogue 168

Romans 8:29-30 (ESV)

For those whom he foreknew he also predestined to be conformed to the image of his Son, in order that he might be the **firstborn among many brothers.**

And those whom he predestined he also called, and those whom he called he also justified, and those whom he justified he also glorified.

INTRODUCTION

My one year old son Judah was sitting on my knee that Sunday morning. I had recently finished my first book *Breath of Life*, and I was sharing one of my favorite revelations with him. Judah was barely a year old, but in that interaction I became aware that a human being's ability to understand deep and transcendent truths need not require experience, or extensive knowledge of language.

I was talking with Judah that morning about his identity. It went on for longer than you might expect, considering the attention span of a one year old.

"Judah, you are my son, but more than that, you are a son of the Father."

He stared at me in a way that indicated he was understanding my words. One year olds don't usually sit still for very long, but he was still.

"Judah, I am your father, but I will never know you as well as our Heavenly Father knows you."

He stared at me in a way that pierced my soul. He smiled and kept looking at me so intently that it almost wrecked me.

"Judah, every time you breathe you declare in a small way, the very Name of God." I inhaled, "YAH…" I exhaled, "WEH."

Judah took the deepest breath I had ever seen him take, repeating it back to me as he now often does, even six months later. "YAH…WEH."

We both laughed, equal parts surprise and hilarity. In a few minutes we were both overwhelmed with joy, laughing in that awkward but fulfilling way that I wish I did more often, as embarrassing as it can be if you aren't with your closest loved ones.

"You are my son, but more than that, you are a son of the Father."

Now my eyes were welling up in tears. It was a spiritual moment between a young father and his only son. It was a significant moment of realization for me as a parent, and I felt the closeness of my heavenly Father in that moment as well.

As I write this today, I am doubly aware of the moments' significance, having buried my earthly father at the end of 2021. My dear and precious father is no longer present on this earth. I would not be the man I am today without his patient care, attention, spiritual guidance, love for the Lord and his personal love and compassion for me, throughout my life. I am a son of the heavenly Father today because I was fathered so well by another one of the Father's sons.

The day that I sat with my son Judah, communicating with him about sonship with our Heavenly Father, was the same day I discovered the deeper meaning in the often told story of Barabbas, the Hebrew prisoner and insurrectionist who was released on Jesus' way to the cross. In Hebrew his name translates quite literally from bar Abba to mean "Son of the father." A layered story filled with revelation for each one of us.

And so this story about sonship began to unfold.

CHAPTER ONE

THE GREAT EXCHANGE OF BARABBAS

Matthew 27:15-17 (MNT)
At festival time the governor was in the habit of releasing any one prisoner whom the crowd chose. At that time they had a notorious prisoner called Jesus Bar-Abbas; so, when they had gathered, Pilate said to them, "Who do you want released? Jesus Bar-Abbas or Jesus the so-called 'Christ'?"

The Jews were familiar with grief and persecution. They were under Roman rule, their most brutal oppressor since Pharaoh had enslaved them in Egypt. But this time the occupation was within their own borders, not in exile or as foreigners in another country. In Jerusalem in those days, centurions were as common as pigeons in the temple pools. Freedom had been replaced by occupation. Fear of their invader was more tangible than hope for deliverance.

What was coming that Friday would prove to be the ultimate inversion. The lives of Jesus Bar-Abbas and Jesus Messiah. One life was destined for a cross and destruction. The other had just been declared their deliverer. One was a reviled, filthy and rejected sinner with no formal education. The other a beloved and often quoted Rabbi, a scholar who not only knew the Torah from memory, but He was actually the author of the Book.

Jesus Bar-Abbas was scorned by his own and probably left for dead by his guerrilla army when the Romans finally foiled their latest coup attempt. He was despised by his enemy, a prisoner that young Roman soldiers would have loved to hate. Kicked at. Punched. Maybe broken a tooth. Some of them lost a friend or even a brother when the zealots raised hell in the city. Now Bar-Abbas was locked behind bars of iron waiting for his time to die. Hoping the resistance might die down, the Romans held Bar-Abbas for longer than the other murderers. The day of his crucifixion would require reinforcements to maintain the uprising of civil disobedience led by the next wave of freedom fighters.

Jesus Messiah was a man of authority and power, with an influence that had not been seen since the holiest prophets had walked through Jerusalem. He was beloved by his own and even respected by many of His would-be enemies. He had just descended upon the City of Jerusalem with a hero's welcome one week earlier, entering the City of David with a procession that harkened to the ceremonious arrival of the Ark of the Covenant centuries earlier when the women, children and elders of Jerusalem watched King David dance with complete abandon before Yahweh.

While the loving welcome of this King had taken place only days earlier, with hooligans now stirring up the mob, it might as well have been ancient history. The same voices that shouted in harmony, "Blessed be the One who comes in the Name of the Lord," now shouted with eery dissonance, "Crucify Him!"

Before we get deeper into the story, you might be wondering at the translation, selected on purpose for its mention of Barabbas' full name. Deep revelation awaits the reader who is able to unpack the text with greater accuracy and depth. The same reason I love studying Hebrew in the Old Testament, as those who have read *Breath of Life* will remember, is why I love to delve into the transcripts and translations and commentaries on the New Testament verses.

Many early transcripts present the full name of Barabbas as none other than "Jesus Barabbas", or in the Hebrew translating into English from "Yahshua, Bar-Abbas," literally naming the criminal in Rome as, "Jesus, son of the Father." Why do many of the more common translations omit this pertinent fact? Maybe it seemed too confusing for the average reader. Perhaps they were unable to discern the full revelation that stood before them.

Yes, the name of Barabbas, the scoundrel of a criminal at the center of the Passover exchange, was Yahshua Bar-abbas which literally means, Jesus son of the Father.

Barabbas and Jesus Christ have the same name.

So in order to distinguish between Jesus, the criminal and insurrectionist that Pilate had in custody, and Jesus, the only begotten Son of the Father, recently hauled before him for questioning by the Jewish priests, Pilate referred to our Savior Jesus as, Yahshua Messiah or Jesus, called the Christ.

Take note of these names, because you will not find a more powerful revelation of salvation and the invitation to sonship, than the one so brilliantly depicted here.

A moment referred to as the great exchange, when a sinner becomes a saved believer, was about to take place. But this time it was being done with a dramatic flair to highlight our Father God's extreme and exceptional love for His chosen.

God the Father, Yahweh, was literally giving us a revelation of His heart for each one of us, whom He affectionately calls, "Sons." There is no clearer sign of the Father's love than this: while we were still sinners, Christ died for us.

Indeed, Barabbas, the man at the heart of the great exchange, was a sinner when Jesus Messiah was exchanged for him. A life for a life. And all four Gospel writers describe the consequential exchange by mentioning the prisoner by name, which calls for our attention as well.

When Jesus Messiah entered the courtyard, the mob was growing in size with word spreading fast through Jerusalem that the Holy Man was being judged in the governor's court. Pontius Pilate was unnerved as he looked down on that massive crowd. There was something about this man Yahshua that disturbed him. His wife had been troubled all of that night, waking him before dawn to share about a righteous man and a series of terrifying dreams she suffered because of Him. Now those dreams of the night had become Pilate's nightmare in the day. A heaviness fell as the supernatural showdown unfolded. This would prove to be the momentous hour of his life. It was the moment he was born for, destined for, and would be remembered for. And he didn't like where it was headed.

Pilate represents a character archetype because of what happened next. The motif or recurrent symbol that Pilate represents is one of negated responsibility.

One of leadership averted. The embodiment of the fear of man. A man who had the authority, but was unwilling to wield it. A man who symbolically washed his hands of Jesus' blood, enabling lesser men to drain the actual life blood from the Messiah's body.

Similarly, but without the global fanfare of Pilate, Barabbas represents the archetype of redemption. His story means so much more for us than Pilate's, when we take a closer look at what transpired next.

It's hard to believe that Pilate still receives more attention than Barabbas by many of the story's tellers and readers. My hope is that this explanation will bring the story of Barabbas to the forefront. Pilate is a key figure in the story, and represents the institutions of our day and the ongoing battle for true leadership in positions of authority.

Shift the lens to Barabbas. The poster boy for rebellion. A man who witnessed broken dreams and broken institutions at work, who undoubtedly suffered because of them. Like the other zealots in his wake, he longed to see change come quickly, was willing to overtake the powerful institutions by force. Lives would be lost, but it would all be for a "greater good."

I love the scene in Risen, the brilliant film by Kevin Reynolds (also the director of other favorites like Count of Monte Cristo, Robin Hood: Prince of Thieves). At the beginning of the film we see a centurion, played by Joseph Fiennes, crushing another Jewish rebellion. One can imagine the followers of Barabbas being among the freedom fighters. There's a poignant scene, where the centurion approaches the leader of this particular uprising. The zealot is already bloodied and wounded, being held down forcibly by two strong Roman warriors. The well-trained soldiers of Rome have quashed another rebellion almost as quickly as it arose. In a final moment of passion the zealot yells at the centurion with believable abandon, "When Messiah comes, Rome will be nothing!"

Equally poignant, the centurion gives pause for only a moment before (we assume) using his blade to knock off the zealot's head. "Until then," he says, wiping the now-silenced freedom fighter's blood from his blade.

I believe the scene paints a reliable picture of what was going on politically at the time. The assets of Rome were spread thin as the empire grew, and her occupants were desperate for change. Not everyone was willing to remain slaves forever. It would be one thing to pay tribute for the benefits of a relatively stable society. But the overlording and taxing nature of Rome, and her vision to dominate the entire world, was forcing the peoples' hand. Not to mention the entire regime was hellbent on removing a moral foundation from the Earth.

Jesus Barabbas was a leader from the opposing camp. He did not embody the Biblical son, with his hands drenched in the blood of his enemies. Mind you, he may have been recalling all the stories of Israel's judges and kings of old. Their hands and robes were stained with blood, too. Barabbas definitely believed in his cause. Why else would he be willing to die for it?

Enter Jesus of Nazareth. He was likely the same age as Jesus Barabbas. While He never raised a finger in violence, His presence stirred the political and spiritual establishment in dramatic ways. Ironically, in his non-violent approach, Jesus called Messiah by His followers, posed a greater threat to the institutions of His day than the violent man, Barabbas.

How could that be? He told the violent to lay down their swords and invited the one receiving the blows to turn the other cheek to their oppressor as well. Yet the Pharisees, king Herod and the Roman establishment all wanted him dead! In a few minutes, they would request that Jesus Barabbas be released in His place, and Jesus Messiah be put to death. The Giver of Life, in exchange for a convicted taker of life.

One question worth asking: did Jesus Barabbas change his name to match this new arrival, Jesus called the Christ, in a willful act of blasphemy? Was Barabbas simply a false teacher and a charlatan trying to paint himself as Messiah instead? Possibly. But I believe that the given name of Barabbas was in fact Jesus (Yahshua) from birth. The reason is fairly simple. According to several sources, Yahshua (in Hebrew meaning 'salvation' and often spelled 'Yeshua' from which we derive the common English name Joshua or Jesse) was a common name among Jews in the time Jesus Christ was on earth. An interesting fact for several reasons. First, it shows us the Jewish people were actively seeking a Savior. They were hungry for deliverance and salvation, to the extent that they were identifying their own children with their burning hope for a prophesied anointed one, Messiah and king.

It also calls to remembrance many Scriptures that the Jews studied regularly in their synagogues at that time. Notably, Isaiah, Jeremiah and other prophets including Daniel all spoke of the restitution of Israel, and when they wrote they often used the word 'yahshua' to speak of the salvation that was coming for the people of God. This is why the angel Gabriel declared to Mary and Joseph that their Son was to be called Yahshua. For He would, "Save His people from their sins." His name meant Salvation. He would embody the prophesied identity of Messiah, by becoming their Savior and Deliverer.

It stands to reason then, that Barrabas' parents would have named their son Jesus at his birth. Identity being so rooted in names within Hebrew culture, Barabbas may have desired to take salvation for the Jews into his own hands, eventually becoming a zealot to fulfill his namesake 'salvation.' Jews placed their identity and calling in their names. So Jesus Barabbas likely believed he was destined to bring freedom to his people. After all, his parents and people shared this generational belief.
Another reason that Matthew's manuscript referring to his first name as Jesus makes sense, is because Bar-Abbas is actually a surname. As when Jesus refers to Peter as "Simon, *Bar-Jonah*", meaning Simon, *son of Jonah*. So Barabbas obviously had another name that the other Gospel writers did not include.

Lastly, Pilate seems to clearly understand the irony when he addresses the people. His comments to the chief priests are soaked in irony. The Jews have been seeking a Savior for generations, long before the arrival of Pilate. At the special Passover Sabbath taking place when Jesus was crucified, Pilate customarily released a Jewish prisoner. The custom already symbolized the prophetic coming Messiah, and how He was a replacement for them, a sacrificial lamb.

So when presenting the crowd and chief priests with their two options, Pilate obviously found some dark humour in the scenario. Do you want to have the lawbreaker and zealot 'savior', Jesus son of Abba? Or do you want this other Jesus, the One who claims to be the actual Son of your Abba in Heaven?

The chief priests were notably offended. Not because Pilate had their names wrong. But because they actually despised Jesus Christ more than the murderer and insurrectionist, Jesus Barabbas. The chief priests wanted a human rebellion, not a heavenly reformation. This also adds creedence to the crowds eventual cries, in one voice, for Jesus Barabbas to be released. Like their spiritual leaders, most of them wanted a human revival. Not a spiritual one.

How many times, like the chief priests and mob inside that courtyard, have we chosen the counterfeit over the real thing? History teaches us well, that claiming or wielding spiritual authority as a humanist tool of manipulation can have dire and overpowering consequences. It can force even the faithful and elect into submission. That is exactly what the ruling leaders did when Jesus Messiah was being tried in the governor's court. The spiritual gurus within Israel in that day were not immune to worldliness or the desires of the flesh, the love of power and control. And the same temptations exist for human beings today, regardless of race or creed. It's easy to claim spiritual authority while wielding human authority. And incredibly dangerous.

After choosing Barabbas instead of Jesus, in a final act of irony, the people in Pilate's courtyard made a potent, self-fulfilling prophetic declaration: "His blood be on us and on our children!"

Matthew 27:25-27

When Pilate saw that he was accomplishing nothing, but that instead a riot was breaking out, he took water and washed his hands before the crowd. "I am innocent of this man's blood," he said. "You bear the responsibility." All the people answered, "His blood be on us and on our children!"

As the imaginary blood washed off Pilate's truly blood-stained hands, an eternal truth was entering the timeline of history. While demons and principalities celebrated their assumed victory over Jesus Christ, the final redemption stake was being lined up to pulverize and obliterate Satan and every past, present and future enemy of Almighty God.

The blood would indeed be on the heads of all the people. From generation to generation. What they

said could not have been more true. An incredible inversion. Declaring their murderous intent, Father God sat on His throne and laughed. Because the blood of His precious Son was pure enough to invert their spirit of murder and release a floodgate of new creation life!

The redemption plan of the Father, Yahweh, officially entered the timeline of human history when Pilate released Barabbas to them and agreed to their outrageous request, to crucify the Lord of Glory in Barabbas' place. Only a good Father can take what looks like the most devastating defeat and use it to complete the greatest victory our world has ever known.

CHAPTER TWO

IN A CELL WITH BARABBAS

Enter the darkness of Barabbas' cell just moments before his release. He's close enough to hear the hum of the growing crowd, which is being stirred into mob mentality madness by the chief priests. But Barabbas isn't close enough to the governor and Caiaphas to hear the orders of Pilate or the voices of the high priests.

He strains to hear what he can through the bars of his cell. Rusty metal, a few tired soldiers, and that awful stench of unwashed prisoners the only barrier between him and another campaign to overturn a Roman regime that he's hated since he was a young boy.

Barabbas is aware of the Jewish Passover festival and Day of Atonement. There's even been chatter inside the prison about which prisoner would win the lottery and earn unmerited freedom. His name has been mentioned more than the other notorious prisoners. Leaning in for clues about what's going on in the courtyard, his fate takes a dramatic turn.

At this distance, Barabbas is stirred by the first shouts of the crowd. In troubling unison, he hears his own name with clarity that vibrates the bars of his rat-infested cell.

"BARABBAS!"

Holding his breath, with goosebumps still rising on his calloused arms and neck, he hears the devastating cry that comes next.

"CRUCIFY HIM!"

The sensation of blood draining from his hungry body. Pins and needles as the cry echoes a second time, "Barabbas! Crucify him!"

It has been decided. Jesus Barabbas, the son of the father chosen to lead the zealot resistance, has been sentenced. He will hang from a tree on the very hill that he wished to dethrone his occupier on. Barabbas crumples into a heap, hands weakly grasping the cold iron, defeated.

A part of him always thought it would end like this. Hoped that his passion, even death, would spark other freedom fighters, culminating in the collapse of the iron empire. At the same time he isn't ready to go. Maybe the violent warrior approach isn't the path to a successful political career. His forefathers David, Gideon and even Samson overcame fierce enemies before him. Why would Yahweh not empower his cause now? Was the God of Israel not mightier than the Roman empire? Believing that he was fighting for the Most High of Israel, surely Father God would fight for him.

No-one could have been more shocked than Barabbas at what happened next. The guards came for him, as expected. The hollow reverberation of his heavy, iron door pivoting. The scrape of metal on metal. Followed by a feeling that only a dead man walking can fully understand. Each step feeling like a countdown. He had only hours left to live. Every breath suddenly felt like a gift. It was the first time that Barabbas actually wanted to be locked inside his cell, maybe for a few more moments, if only to quiet himself and have enough time to say a prayer.

But Barabbas had missed the rest of the conversation. Play back the tape from inside the courtyard. You can find the full exchange in Matthew 27.

Pilate (quietly compared with the yelling mob): Who do you want me to release for you: Jesus Barabbas, or Jesus who is called Christ?

The Crowd (shouting): Barabbas!

Pilate (again asking, for he knew their motives were envious): Which of the two do you want me to release to you?

The Crowd (shouting all the louder): BARABBAS!

Pilate (his voice shaking with quiet dread): Then what shall I do with Jesus the Christ?

The Crowd (shouting as one): CRUCIFY HIM!

Barabbas believed, as he was hauled out of his cell, that he was the one sentenced to be crucified. For indeed, from his vantage point, he would have heard only the fierce cries of the mob. His name. And the sentence of death. "Barabbas! Crucify him!"

Oh the look in Jesus Messiah's eyes when Barabbas walked by! Envy and jealousy were not feelings Jesus Christ possessed. So when Jesus Barabbas caught the eyes of the true Jesus, he was gazing at the essence of pure love. Unbroken, unfettered, unrelenting, unbelievable love.

This same Jesus Messiah had already called other zealots to be His disciples. He had a heart for their passion, however misguided. He redirected their zeal to His Father in Heaven.

There are moments of significance in our lives where time just seems to slow down. Trauma can cause this sensation, but life-altering beauty can cause it too. Scientific theories have been proposed, and there is one theory that seems to fit this instance just right.

When there is a dramatic increase in a person's internal processes, actual events around that person can seem to take place in slow motion.

Surely, at the great exchange between Yahshua Barabbas and Yahshua Messiah this phenomena took place. Neurons firing, anxiety overloading, shock taking over one son of the father's physical body. Suddenly the sound drowns out, only a subtle ringing in his ears. Barabbas can feel his own heart beat. He is looking into human eyes, but there is another Spirit behind those eyes that he has desired to gaze upon. He is looking into the eternal eyes of Christ, the Messiah that he longed for, searched for, and ultimately believed would only appear to rescue a future generation.

The Ancient One, embodied in flesh, now before him. Not only before him, but exchanging His precious life for his embittered soul. A son of the father. Set free by the Son of the Father.

Whether time slowed down in reality or not, in the spirit realm thrones and spiritual darkness were all at once being shaken. This changed everything. Past, present and future. Redemption through the Fathers' Son Jesus came down from Heaven like a boulder upon the glass construct of the enemy's grip on the world. Precisely obliterating every stronghold and lie. Shattering evil into a billion pieces.

And the best part about the inversion was that the enemies of God didn't even know it was taking place.

Sometimes we hear the stories from the Bible so often that they become familiar to us. We have a certain view of them, because we've imagined the story a certain way, or heard the story told by a pastor or teacher or filmmaker.

Insert yourself into Barabbas' sandals for a moment. See it from a new angle. He was worthy of death. He was not a true son of the Father at this moment in the story. On the contrary, he was a murderer, criminal and insurrectionist. Big words. We could just call him a sinner.

There is a word we can all relate to. If we were sitting down for coffee right now together, not a soul reading these words would truthfully deny the presence of shame, guilt, fear, anxiety, or some other similar emotion or trauma that exists in, has impacted, your own life. Sin simply means 'missing the mark.' How many of us honestly believe that if we are the arrow in the archery of life, we have been able to hit the target every single time? Shame, guilt, fear, lust, lying, envy, doubt, pain, addiction, trauma, and the many other words we know too well as human beings have caused us to miss the target. We truly have *all* missed the mark. Even when we had the best intentions and tried our very best, we missed the mark.

We will never hit the target every time without Christ. The story of Jesus Barabbas, a son of the father, teaches us this. And in the most cinematic inversion that I can see in all the Scriptures, Jesus Messiah turned the table.

The great exchange is a revelation for the saved and unsaved because it shows us with stunning immediacy, that while we were still sinners Christ died for us. And not only that, but He died so that we could be exchanged from lost sinners and sons of this age, to saved believers, and sons of the Father.

It took the true Son of the Heavenly Father to redeem us. But there would be no need for redemption and the inversion of darkness, unless there remained lost sons on the earth.

If humanity needs no Savior, the Son of the Creator of the Universe died for nothing. The overarching message of the Bible, and this short book, is that Jesus *did die for something*.

Jesus died for lost souls like Barabbas. He exchanged Himself for us. We are Barabbas. We are lost sons. Until we pass by Jesus Messiah and look into those beautiful eyes. Until we realize that we were worthy of death, but we have been saved into life.

I believe salvation captured Barabbas that day. To be at the center of a moment called the great exchange, and not be set free? That doesn't seem possible to me.

I pray that you apply the power of the great exchange in your own life today. Barabbas heard the crowd yelling, "Crucify him!" But God the Father said, "I will save him in exchange for My own Son. I will take Barabbas and make him a newborn son of the Father."

What are you hearing the crowds, the world or the enemy yelling in your ears? Is it about your value (or lack thereof)? Is it a lie about your identity? Is it a curse about your ability, gifts or success? Is it that all too familiar mocking voice, maybe even your own inner voice, trying to bury yourself again, saying you aren't valuable enough or worthy of God's love?

Heap that shame upon Jesus Messiah. That is the reason why He died. Barabbas did it. I don't know for sure, but I imagine that when the moment was unfolding he didn't even know it yet. He had been saved. He had been exchanged from death into life. And he had been bought at an unbelievable price.

So take the walk towards the cross like Barabbas did. It's a pilgrimage for one and all, and an invitation to die to yourself. Die to sin, die to the things of this world, die to your own wants, needs and desires. But then, like Christ, you will be resurrected. If you will turn your pain, shame and every trauma over to the Son of the Father and admit that you have missed the mark. Invite the true Son of God in, and you will become a born again son of the Father yourself.

CHAPTER THREE

SONSHIP AS A THEME IN SCRIPTURE

There are several key themes within Scripture that emerge if we take the time to study the text from beginning to end. While some themes are obvious, others are hidden in plain sight. If a theme emerges steadily enough, and we take the time to meditate on it, the significance of that theme becomes difficult to shake.

One Biblical theme that has rocked me to the core, is the theme of Breath, which I wrote about in my first book. Breath, and specifically the 'Breath of God' keep coming for humanity throughout the Biblical narrative. First, when God breathed upon Adam and Eve in the garden to bring them to life. Breath continues to appear throughout Genesis, Exodus and Ezekiel, too. In the Gospel accounts, Jesus breathed His last breath as a breath of redemption from the cross, and soon after He breathed the Holy Spirit from His own lungs into His disciples in the upper room.

Another theme that we can not avoid from the beginning to the end of Scripture, is the theme of sonship.

Sonship:
The *right* relationship of son to father.

The relationship between the Heavenly Father and His children is the central theme of the entire Bible. I challenge you to consider if there is any theme in Scripture more important to both God and humanity than sonship. The creation narrative is based on it. The salvation narrative is based on it. And the new creation narrative is based on it too. Basically sonship comes up as the theme of the past, the present and the future.

Romans 8:19
For the whole creation hopes for and expects the revelation of the sons of God.

The parent-child relationship is referred to with the catch-all title of sonship, but it applies to both men and women, boys and girls because the children of God are all defined Scripturally as 'sons'. Sonship first arrives on page one in Genesis with the creation of Adam. Adam is even labeled "the son of God" in the Biblical genealogy found in Luke which outlines the arrival of Jesus, tracing his human heritage all the way back to Adam.

Sonship is a primary theme in the flood story of Genesis, where the Bible says the sons of God had relationships with the daughters of men. In that story we learn that even angels' relationship with God is most accurately understood by pointing out their relationship as sons to a father.

Sonship is the core theme in the life of Abraham who is selected from the peoples of the world to be God's son, ultimately leading to the establishment of the nation of Israel who are collectively labeled God's son throughout the Bible. Then, in order to fulfill his own destiny, Abraham and Sarah have to (supernaturally) birth their own son in the story to take hold of the promises of God. They have to pass their own inheritance to humanity, through a son.

Sonship is also a key theme in the story of Exodus, culminating in the deliverance of God's chosen people (again Israel is called God's son), while the climax of the ten plagues results in the firstborn sons of Egypt being tragically killed because of Pharaoh's disobedience.

King Saul, Israel's first king, is a tragic tale that reveals how we can miss the mark as one of God's chosen sons, and King David's story is the antithesis, and he later receives the promise that one of his sons will sit on the throne of God's Kingdom forever.

The prophesies of major and minor prophets including Ezekiel, Isaiah, Jeremiah and more, all talk about the promised Son of Man, Who is going to come into the world.

Notably, with the birth of Jesus and the start of His ministry on earth, sonship is the primary theme, too. Jesus reveals through His life and ministry that He is the **Son of God**. He also refers to Himself as the **Son of Man**. What the two titles collectively mean are that Jesus is fully God and fully human. Both His divinity and humanity are most clearly understood in His relationship to God and humanity as a Son.

There are also more than a dozen key stories in the Gospels that have to do with sonship. Most are even more poignant because they are narrated by Jesus, the Son of the Father.

We have the parable of the Prodigal Son, then the Land Owner who sends his one and only son to make things right when the bad guys have taken over. Later Jesus gets into an argument with the Jews who first claim to be sons of Abraham, then raise the stakes by claiming to be sons of God, but ultimately gain the label 'sons of the Devil' when Jesus points out they are serving Satan rather than the Heavenly Father.

The Bible is like an unfolding thriller all about sonship! Why is this such a key theme?

It's there to draw us, provoke us and invite us to get desperate before our Father, and learn about our true identity as His sons. Not only to be children who are related to human parents by birth, but to actually understand what God means when He says, "You are my son."

Because your true identity is not only as a natural son (or daughter) but your true identity is that you are invited to be a son of God! This identity label is the most important truth for you to understand in your daily life.

That deserves repeating. Your identity as a son of God, is the most important truth for you to understand in your daily life. It will literally change everything you say and do for the better. Once you understand it, sonship will lift you from the mud and mire and place you in the right seat, the one that Jesus invited you to sit in with Him.

JI Packer wrote a famous book called Knowing God. I found an amazing quote from his book that states, "If you want to judge how well a person understands Christianity, find out how much he makes of the thought of being God's child, and having God as his

Father. If this is not the thought that prompts and controls your worship and prayers and your whole outlook on life, it means that you do not understand Christianity very well at all."

Goosebumps. Did you know that many of the great leaders of the faith ultimately came to *sonship* as the topic of greatest significance for the saved believer? Naturally, to begin with, we look to Salvation in Christ (the Father's Son). But from there, in order to live and move and have our being in alignment with the things of God, we need to understand our own personal identities as sons of the Father.

The truths about sonship from Scripture come with an open invitation to the daughters of faith, not just the men. The theme of sonship applies to both sons and daughters because the theme of sonship is a spiritual theme. So while we look to the physical traits of a son for direction, ultimately sonship can only be fully understood spiritually.

One of my prayers as I use human language to write this book, is that the women reading it will not be left behind because of the semantics of 'son' even though I will repeat that word over and over. The Bible does the same thing, because the concept is meant to be understood with spiritual eyes, not human ones.

This book will focus on key stories about Jesus, the Son of God and Son of Man, to unveil some key revelations about sonship. Before we get there, remember how the creation of the universe, and the world we live in, climaxed with the creation of a son? When God the Father got to the pinnacle of His creation, what was it He made? Or rather, who was it He made?

Here is where I stumbled upon my first revelation. The Most High God of all creation could have labeled any work of art His masterpiece. There can only be one masterpiece in any artist's collection. God the Father doesn't shape a clay pot, a mug or a bowl. He doesn't crack through tectonic plates and make Mt. Everest His masterpiece, or label any iconic landmark, structure or land mass His masterpiece. We look around and there is so much beauty in creation itself. He doesn't even make the angels or divine beings that we learn about in the Book of Revelation and label them His masterpiece.

There is a singular focal point in His mind when it comes to creating the *greatest of all His works*.

God was not satisfied with an inanimate object when He arrived at the pinnacle of His work as a creative artist. No, when the score came to crescendo and He chose to unveil His

masterpiece, God made a son. He made Adam, the first son of the Father.

Luke 3:38
Adam was the son of God.

Think of Adam's arrival on the scene this way: Adam is the first reason why humanity is invited to actually call Yahweh our Father! Because Yahweh is the actual father of Adam. Yahweh gets his hands dirty in the mud of the Garden, making a man, and soon after a woman, in His very own image. Which is what we have the incredible ability to do as human parents. We continue the story. We do what God did. We make human beings in our own image. Making human beings that resemble us, not only in appearance, but in character. They are not only similar to us in bodily form, but we pass on intangible things to our children, too. Spiritual, emotional and personality traits.

We are not merely a physical body as the humanists would try to convince you to believe. No. We are also a soul and we have a spirit.

When Adam takes his first breath, and becomes a living soul, there is something innately spiritual about him. God, His Father molds him from the dust and clay and says, "You are going to be like I am." When

God's breath, which is His living spirit, was blown on Adam, Adam transformed from something that was merely physical. A lump of matter that was truly inanimate suddenly became a living, spiritual being.

And quite shockingly, in the same way that God created Adam with this spiritual nature, we are now enabled to create offspring. Sons and daughters who are also spiritual beings. And as much as we understand our physical traits as children, there is a spiritual parallel that is simultaneously at work in each one of us. As a human being, your spiritual self is invited by the Father of us all, to be a son of God!

This is epic. There is a physical plane operating simultaneously *with* a spiritual plane. And physically you are the son of a human father and mother. But in the spirit realm, you have a Father as well. And He wants you to become His son in a real and permanent and eternal way.

The first statement Yahweh, Adam's Father, made about him points us to the root and foundation of sonship. When Yahweh saw who He had made, after creating Adam and Eve, the Father profoundly stated, 'they are very good.' In other words, when He saw the order and the beauty of human children bearing His image, He spoke of His pleasure over them. He was proud of His kids.

They were in right relationship to their Father. Their relationship to one another was very good. That is the essence of sonship. By definition, sonship is about the right relationship between father and son.

Have you ever seen the pride and joy on the face of new parents? Perhaps you've had the privilege of holding your own son or daughter in your hands? I dare say it's a spiritual experience every single time. You can not truly believe, if you've held that precious life in your hands and stared into those glassy clear eyes, that nothing spiritual is taking place. The image of God in your grasp is a precious and holy gift. It's very good. I think when we hold a new baby in our arms we are flashing back to that moment Yahweh first shared with Adam and Eve in the Garden of Eden. For a moment, as we treasure that life that we cradle with a love unmatched since the creation of the world, we understand the meaning of sonship.

As the only begotten Son of the Father, the life of Jesus is our university for sonship. It's actually a bit like sonship for dummies. When I re-read the stories of Jesus with the theme of sonship in mind, I feel like a dummy myself, as the clarity of the theme of sonship jumps off the page.

I invite you to read the life of Jesus in the Gospels again this month. See if you find the power of His identity as Son of God more powerful than ever, when viewing His choices, His ministry and His miracles through the lens of sonship. Even the way He prays to His Father makes it so clear that Jesus is a Son and He knows His identity. As we learn from the definition of sonship, it's all about being in right relationship. Jesus consistently demonstrates what it means to be in right relationship with the Father.

CHAPTER FOUR

THE LAST MINUTE BELIEVER ON THE CROSS

There are several stories in Scripture dotting the map on the road to our ultimate destination of *becoming sons*. None of the Biblical stories are recorded without reason. As another 3:16 verse teaches us, "*All* Scripture is God-breathed and is useful for teaching, rebuking, correcting and training in righteousness…" 2 Timothy 3:16 NIV

After the salvation of Barabbas, the man exchanged for Christ at the festival of Passover, Jesus walked to Calvary along with two convicted criminals. Unlike Jesus, we learn in the Scriptures by their own confession, that these men were deserving of death. They were both thieves, and ultimately they carried their crosses to Skull Mountain bearing the punishment and responsibility for their crimes.

What's most remarkable about their story, may be revealed by the simple message in their dialogue with Jesus that many of us have probably overlooked.

Sometimes our familiarity with a story or concept cause us to miss the basic truth staring us right in the face. I admit this was my own experience as I re-read the story after studying it more thoroughly in recent months. Like many of the Gospel stories, I've read them dozens of times, in different translations and seasons of life. I've also read the coinciding stories from the four Gospels to compare notes from the accounts of Matthew, Mark, Luke and John. Sometimes the details differ or there are additional insights from one of them, helping us understand a particular story better.

In the process of revisiting the final day in the life of Jesus, I was drawn to three stories as Christ walked to His mount of crucifixion. Three men, two I believe were Jews and one was a Gentile, received salvation from Jesus on the way there. The name Yahshua literally means 'salvation.' So, while the embodiment of Salvation made His way to Golgotha, salvation inevitably overtook more than a few lost souls. Several are recorded for our benefit.

Salvation even arrived as Jesus breathed His last breaths in the flesh. Hanging from a tree, arms spread wide open in love, His message was clear. "I will embrace any lost soul willing to look to Me." One of the souls we'll study in the next chapter actually received salvation after Jesus died (and before He rose again). Even a dead Jesus was able to release new life and salvation.

We've covered Barabbas, the archetype of redemption. Next, we will look at the thief on the cross. Perhaps we can call him, "the archetype of repentance."

Mark 15:27
Along with Jesus, they crucified two robbers, one on His right and one on His left.

Matthew 27:44
In the same way, even the robbers who were crucified with Him berated Him.

The Gospel of Luke adds a truly intriguing nuance to the story. Did the Gospel writers' versions differ because Matthew and Mark weren't physically present at the time of the crucifixion? Or perhaps not present for the climactic moment. Maybe, by even greater grace than we can comprehend, after berating Jesus himself, the penitent thief changed his tune.

As I read the stories again, that version made the most sense to me. In the Book of James we learn how the same tongue that curses God can offer worship and blessing to Him as well. When we unpack the moments in succession, we start to see how the discipleship of the repentant thief may have transpired, within only a few short hours of knowing Jesus.

The witness of *how* Jesus died was a testimony enough for many to believe. How Jesus was born was a miracle, the only child born of a virgin. How Jesus lived was a miracle, the only man who lived without sin. His resurrection was the greatest miracle in human history.

But the way Jesus died was also a miracle. He didn't revile a soul, not even the men who sliced open every pore and vein with the cat of nine tails. The flogging alone was enough to kill a man.

He didn't curse the sorriest of Roman soldiers who drove Him on relentlessly even as every last drop of stamina drained from His bleeding body on the route to the Skull.

He didn't break from right relationship with His Father or revile any divine beings or angels for letting the punishment continue. Remember, He went willingly.

He didn't even put the chief priests, teachers of the law or self-righteous Pharisees in their place when they mocked Him moment after moment as He hung there, fading out as surely as the darkening sun, when creation itself nearly collapsed under the weight of Messiah's death.

As the two thieves (known from antiquity as Dismas and Gestas) mocked Him, Jesus didn't rebuke or obliterate them either. The man known as 'the good thief,' may have only had a momentary flash of revelation. That moment would prove to be all that was needed to set himself apart from 'the bad thief,' on a path from terminal death to everlasting salvation.

Fittingly, the band *Third Day* wrote a song that I love about this very subject. It's not too cryptic in it's title: *Thief*. There are many poignant lyrics in the song which begins:

I am a thief, I am a murderer
Walkin' up this lonely hill
What have I done?
No, I don't remember
And no one knows just how I feel

In the final hours, or as Scripture poignantly confirms, during the final breaths of Jesus, Dismas had a change of heart.

I wonder if Yahshua would have given up His spirit sooner, had Dismas repented more quickly? Did Jesus suffer for several more hours, waiting for the moment to arrive?

As the life of the Living God faded, a transformation took place in one of the two thieves. It's almost too cinematic to believe, but it's true, and confirmed in Luke's Gospel.

Luke 23: 39-43,

One of the criminals who hung there heaped abuse on Him. "Are You not the Christ?" he said. "Save Yourself and us!" But the other one rebuked him, saying, "Do you not even fear God, since you are under the same judgment? We are punished justly, for we are receiving what our actions deserve. But this man has done nothing wrong." Then he said, "Jesus, remember me when You come into Your kingdom!"

And Jesus said to him, "Truly, I tell you, today you will be with Me in Paradise."

Moments later. Breaths later. Jesus gave up His spirit. The Son gave His true eternal self back to the Father in Heaven. But not until one more soul was added to the Kingdom. One more *son*.

What Grace! Many of us have heard a story of decisive repentance, or even heard about a sudden turnaround on a persons' death bed. This was that moment! Poignant, piercing, powerful and poetic. While the righteous Pharisees looked on, a rebellious thief became a son of the Father. Then they broke his legs and he suffocated to death. But not without the purest anticipation of Glory that was only one *breath* away.

As I read the story in Luke's Gospel it clicked for me in a new way. The thief known traditionally as Gestas saw what the crowd said and did, he heard the words of the mockers and added his voice to the chaos. He asked to come *down*. *Down* from the cross, *down* from certain death, *down* to the earth he knew so well.

But when Dismas caught Jesus' eyes, His eyes still ablaze with a flicker of fire, he realized something far greater than any momentary miracle could accomplish. Coming down from the cross would only lead, ultimately, to a timely or untimely death. The world was not enough.

Dismas looked at Jesus receiving the mocking blows and heard the cries of a dying man without curses on His lips, without fear of the shame, without human will to live for earth's sake. *He saw Jesus looking up*, and realized he and the other thief had wasted almost every second of their lives looking *down*.

I believe that was the turning point. Belief took hold of him, and his heart was gripped with unstoppable conviction. He changed his tune. And sang a salvation song instead.

The lyrics from the Third Day song continue:

O who is this man, this man beside me
That they call the King of the Jews?
No, they don't believe that He's the Messiah
But somehow, I know that it's true

O they laugh at Him in mockery
And beat Him 'til He bleeds
O they nail Him to the rugged cross
And raise Him, yeah, they raise Him up next to me

My time has come, I'm slowly fading
But I deserve what I receive
Jesus when You enter Your kingdom
Could Ya please, please remember me?

O He looks at me still holdin' on
And the tears fall from His eyes
And He says, "I tell the truth
O today, O you will live with me in Paradise!"

We can waste our entire lives, like Gestas, looking *down*. Or we can turn our eyes and our hearts heavenward to Christ, and like Dismas, look *up*.

Our hope, our future, our Garden of Eden is there. Once we gain access by faith, we will not only know that we're destined to reign forever. But when we learn, and indeed know in our spirits that sonship places us in the Heavenly seat with Christ, we will begin to bring Heaven down.

CHAPTER FIVE

THE CENTURION'S DECLARATION OF FAITH

There was another man between the crosses while Jesus died. Born in Rome, his most important post was in Jerusalem. He was charismatic, strong, and rose in the ranks of the iron army. Before long, his strengths were noted by his superiors. Effective in battle, he earned the respect of his fellow soldiers. After more than a decade, spent mostly in a suit of armour working relentlessly for the empire, he was promoted from overseeing a small company, to the coveted role of centurion. A captain of the army, hardened in the discipline of military service and combat. He had proven his qualities of leadership. He was commissioned to carry out orders.

Overseeing eighty to a hundred soldiers, he earned more pay. But more than ever, his life became his duty. Servant to an emperor he would never meet. A small cog in the nearly global Roman empire, he served knowing that in many ways, he would never truly benefit from his dedication. He would probably die in a future battle, or more likely, the next insurrection. But the job paid, he never went hungry, and in a Roman soldier's world, centurion was almost as good a dream as you could ever live for.

He earned money from career, respect from his peers and even honor from his superiors. But serving the kingdom of this world did not produce inner peace. Killing for a living, he found no certainty of his place in the universe where, deep down, he believed there was a Creator, perhaps even a God in heaven.

Over time the doubt grew to emptiness in his spirit. A void as vast and dark as the quiet vacuum of space. His inner longing came with one age-old question burning inside. Like kerosene in the lantern of his heavy-laden soul, steadily humming, always putting out the faintest crack of light. Is there anything more to life than this?

Nothing could prepare him, or any one of us, for that day. The sun rose like every other. The stench of malnourished soldiers in the barracks. The tireless call of duty. A long list of tasks to do before another exhaustion-fuelled sleep.

According to his captain, this was going to be a great day for the men. A morale boost to break the monotony. Today their duty was to perform an unexpected crucifixion. Today was an open invitation to mutilate and murder another Jew. The Colosseum would come a generation later, but the bloodsport didn't wait for her arrival. The first gladiators were the centurions themselves, torturing and crucifying thousands, tens of thousands, in a few short years.

Dissidents, whether proven or simply labeled 'criminals' by local magistrates, were taken to the most well-traveled roads to be put on display, hung on rough hewn trees carved into posts, staked into the ground like pegs for a dwelling. Only these posts held human bodies, living souls burdened with shame and raised up to be seen by every traveler and pilgrim on the road to Jerusalem. Elevated so they could be mocked while they breathed a few, final, shallow breaths.

But for a Roman soldier, a crucifixion provided a brief escape from the more tiresome work of night time patrols, house raids and the danger of the battlefield. The centurion even felt a spark of joy, if you could call it that, when he received the call. When you live in a cycle of boredom and misery, even bloodsport excites your darkened soul. The Scripture confirms it, for while overseeing his men, this centurion allowed some of the most vile moments recorded in the torture of Christ.

Then the soldiers led Jesus away into the palace (that is, the Praetorium) and called the whole company together. They dressed Him in a purple robe, twisted together a crown of thorns, and set it on His head. And they began to salute Him: "Hail, King of the Jews!"

Mark 15: 16-20,

They kept striking His head with a staff and spitting on Him. And they knelt down and bowed before Him. After they had mocked Him, they removed the purple robe and put His own clothes back on Him. Then they led Him out to crucify Him.

Taking him before an entire company, not just 100 men, but 600 men, the vilest of the bunch arose. And the centurion either allowed, or participated in, the vulgar exchange. Aware of the reports of miracles, power and authority over demons, the centurion threw his hand up not in an act of worship or surrender, but in the rock-hard shape of a fist, to add to the bloody blows.

He watched, or perhaps held the staff himself, first positioned to malign Jesus' rulership and authority, then pulled away to be swung at His head. Not once.

But over and over again. Until the light of the world's own eyes grew dim.

If that wasn't enough, this centurion encouraged the rowdy bunch to strip Jesus, gather up His kingly robes and play a game. Indeed, gambling and wagering and betting on Jesus' very life. How many more breaths? How many more hours? Who will die first, the King or the thieves?

The Maker of the elements, the Author of Life, allowed His lost and prodigal children to abuse Him using the very devices He once created. And He did so willingly.

This centurion was well aware as the beatings drew on, that something was terribly amiss. Most of the fun the soldiers enjoyed came from the groaning, screaming, wailing agony of their prey. The begging, the pleading, the grovelling in search of one shred of humanity. They would never get mercy, but the soldiers loved how they begged for it. And they always did. Humanity at its most awful surfaces in times of pain. And crucifixion was the apex of suffering in the Roman's Godless world.

But like a sheep before the shearer is silent, this man, Jesus, didn't even open His mouth. Except to adjust His teeth, swallow some blood, and receive another blow. It continued as the cool of morning faded into the hot swelter of Jerusalem by noon. That was one of the first moments the centurion felt his soul lurch within him. More violent than the wrenching twist of a stomach purging itself of poisoned food, the centurion's eyes met with Jesus' eyes at the very moment, when all at once the burning sun of midday, went black.

As God was his witness, the centurion felt his own wavering spirit tremble more surely than the earthquake that would soon follow. He testified, not with his words quite yet, but with his inner man, that the world was under a curse. And like all of us, his own hand was on the gavel, bringing down the crushing force of pronounced justice upon no-one but himself. Who was the offender? This other-worldly man who spoke no curse over his violent persecutors?

For a moment, the centurion had the panicked feeling that King David had, after condemning himself before Nathan the prophet in the hall of justice in Jerusalem, teetering as he did on the edge of his rule, feeling the evaporation of his anointed reign. When David, the great giant killer said those words, it nearly toppled his own throne, and the golden sceptre of his authority along with it. For when confronted with the sin of a certain man in Israel, David pronounced a sure and righteous judgment.

David burned with anger against the man and said to Nathan: "As surely as Yahweh lives, the man who did this deserves to die! Because he has done this thing and has shown no pity, he must pay...four times over."

Then Nathan said to David, "You are that man!" (2 Samuel 12: 5-7 BSB)

The microphone may have never dropped harder, for the prophet spoke the undeniable truth. For the first time in his dutiful life, the centurion wondered at the mysterious power of sin. Sin itself, that ancient entity and enemy of humanity, was approaching its climax. Jesus and His followers were under attack. The very redemption plan of Almighty God appeared to be falling apart.

The enemies were encamped around Him. The hypocritical religious leaders now surrounded Jesus like a pack of wolves. The ever-bloodthirsty Roman regime, the empire that crushed any sign of uprising almost as quickly as it appeared would have her fill, like Babylon the great whore, always blaspheming, always thirsty for a goblet of pure and precious blood.

But the centurion still had doubts. Why had even Jesus' closest friends and followers abandoned him? Why weren't they fighting to the death to ransom His life? Suddenly the slow motion silence at the onset of that midday darkness was broken by a series of screams. Panicked that one of the three cross-carriers might somehow escape, the centurion made orders. Torches were somehow lit, soldiers somehow pressed back the crowds, the final steps to the mount of Golgotha were somehow completed. It was nearing the historic hour of Jesus' last breath. And the centurion's next few decisions became the unconscious motions of an experienced executioner.

To say the next three hours felt like an eternity would be putting it lightly. Each event that unfolded proved the only moment more potent than the last. For one moment after another, the centurion soldier witnessed the unflinching brilliance of Jesus. He said no curse to the religious leaders, the foreign passersby, or even the bloodied criminals on his right and left who berated Him. Then, at the centurion's witness, He invited the blaspheming villain on his right to join him in Paradise.

After the exchange between the thieves and Jesus, the centurion watched one of his officers win the purple robe in a game of dice, gambling for Christ's invaluable mantle. It was indeed a kingly robe, woven without seam. Such raiment brought into question the claims of the priests and teachers of the law cursing Him. This was indeed no mere peasant seeking to rise in the cabal of Jewish leadership. Perhaps He was their true King.

The centurion wondered at how his soldier valued the robe so richly, all the while abusing and spitting on the living soul Who wore it. A kingly robe, yes, but surely only a trifle compared to the value of a human being.

There are moments when life becomes so foreign, so much different than you believed it to be. Your existence, as you knew it, comes into question. Like the first time, when you were a child, you overheard a news report about a local man abusing or kidnapping a child in your neighborhood. Or the realization that slavery and exploitation exist in your own town, or witness a drug deal on the street corner across from your family's church. It shatters the belief, maybe even your hope, that the world is truly safe. At the very least, it's not entirely *good*.

As he watched his soldiers, the centurion slipped from his role as executioner into an out-of-body fly on the wall surveying the events. Then he realized, everything was about to change. His world could no longer be the same. Because the world was in fact, no longer the same. And then He said those words. Those unbelievable, earth-shaking words. They hit harder than a blow to the face, a punch to the stomach, a graze of a knife on the thigh or forearm. All of which the centurion had felt before.

"Father, forgive them. They don't know what they are doing."

He was right. The centurion hadn't a God-blessed clue. What was he doing? He would reflect upon it for the rest of his life. And the world along with him. Had he done the unthinkable? Misjudged the Savior of the world, for a criminal worthy of a savage death? Had he disfigured and marred beyond human likeness the Author of Life? Were his orders responsible for suffocating the Giver of Breath?

The earth was still shaking when the centurion responded. I imagine that his personal journal may have been filled with these words:

Indeed, I, the centurion am one of the handful of human beings who watched Jesus breathe His last breath. I was undone then, as I am now, equally shaken each time I recall the events of that unbelievable day. For after witnessing His compassion, even for the criminals that hung with Him, berating Him, I heard His faltering voice call upon His Father in Heaven, and ask for God to forgive us.

I was the man overseeing the spikes that pierced His hands and feet. And even though my hand was still on the hammer that split through His tender bones, even though His blood was still wet against my skin, I was the one He spoke to. I felt a gaze of compassion from Him that my own father and mother had never given.

They say He looked out at the crowd when He said it, but in my memory, it was a man arms open, heart exposed, looking straight at me. Yes, His eyes were on me alone. After He said 'Father forgive them,' I heard Him add, 'And Father, make this soldier another one of your sons. I want him to be my brother. I don't want to spend a day in eternity without him.'

The earth was still shaking when I responded. I am grateful that the Gospel writers heard my utterance, for it was more true a word than I had ever spoken to that day, or will ever speak again. From eternity past to eternity present, there may never be a truer word spoken in all the universe.

"Truly. This Man. Was the Son of *GOD*."

Later on, Jesus' followers would share the centurion's words. How the book of the Law in Leviticus stated thousands of years earlier: *For the life of the flesh is in the blood: and I have given it to you upon the altar to make an atonement for your souls: for it is the blood that makes atonement for the soul.*

When the earth shook, the veil that was torn in the temple in Jerusalem, which suddenly revealed the Holy of Holies, made entrance possible for any son or daughter who believed in Jesus. It was by the death of Jesus on the cross that the veil, which again, hid and concealed and rightly covered the entrance to the Holy of Holies, was rent from top to bottom. That was the veil beyond which no man could enter; the veil beyond which the high priest could penetrate only once a year on the Day of Atonement. The veil beyond which dwelt the Spirit of God.

And the revelation of sonship to be taken from the centurion's testimony is one that beckons every lost soul to look up at Christ like that man did. For before the veil was torn, God had been hidden. Not a soul on earth truly knew what God was like. By the death of Jesus we see the hiddenness of God, finally and beautifully manifested. The face of God and His purely redemptive love was all at once on display. Once barred to all men, in the tearing of the veil, Salvation, the namesake of Yahshua Himself, was now available to all.

The renting of the veil showed to man *what* God is like, *how* man can enter into the presence of God, and *Who* God really is. Have you let the veil come down in your own life? You might have done so to a degree, but have you let the scales fall away completely from your natural and fleshly and human eyes? To truly gaze upon Christ, is to see the Son of Father God in the flesh in the same way the centurion did. And when you see Him, and acknowledge that He is the Son of the Father, you become a son of the

Father, too. And as you follow Him, you can be sure that you are on an incredibly transformative path to becoming like Him. You are continually transformed until your transformation will be completed. That will happen when we all meet Him together, face to face.

Beloved, we are God's children now, and what we will be has not yet appeared; but we know that when he appears we shall be like him, because we shall see him as he is.
1 John 3:2 (ESV)

Like the centurion, at that moment we will finish the journey to becoming true sons. Forever.

CHAPTER SIX

THREE WOMEN WHO HELPED DEFINE SONSHIP

God the Father created our mothers and He holds each of them in a special place within His heart. Our earthly mothers teach us so much about the world and nurture us after bringing us into existence. The love between a mother and her child is one of the most powerful bonds that exists on the earth.

Motherhood is also a more prominent theme in Scripture than we often see at first glance. There are some stand out women, and mothers, in the Bible that teach us a lot about sonship. Beyond that, we would not have any of the outstanding men and heroes of the faith that we look up to, without their influential and Holy Spirit-filled mothers.

Studying Godly mothers in both the Old and New Testament reveals a few powerful themes. There are three mothers in the Biblical narrative who become even more prominent when studying Biblical sonship. While there are at least seven mothers in Scripture who I am personally inspired by, I want to focus on three of them.

All three of their stories begin with the same seed. The seed of promise. The seed of calling.

When Yahweh spoke to the first mother who walked the earth, Eve, after the fall of humanity in the Garden of Eden, He started by giving her a promise. He promised her that she and her offspring would crush the head of humanity's mortal and supernatural enemy. I find this truth fascinating - the theme of promise continues in our lives today. We are still receiving the good promises of God that were given to our ancestors, and still passing on new promises from God to our children.

God is seeking fathers and mothers. More than that, He longs to raise them up to be His own precious sons and daughters. It's another inversion of the upside-down Kingdom of God. To be kingdom-functioning parents, we are called to be kingdom sons and daughters. According to the Book of Chronicles, the Father's eyes are not just meandering here or there, but *His eyes are roaming throughout the entire earth to strengthen (and give promises) to the ones fully committed to him.* (2 Chronicles 16:9)

The Father is giving promises to his children. It's one of the things He does, and He does it well. When it comes to receiving a promise there is always a theme that emerges. Something happens every single time, at least from my experience, and according to what I see in the pattern of Scripture.

After the joy and delight of receiving a promise, you can set your watch by the fact that there is going to be resistance. Almost immediately after a good word is given, spoken and released, we either experience a delay, a roadblock or a stalling in the actualization of our promise.

I'm sure there are some promises that have been given and fulfilled quickly, but I think if we look at most of our own lives and if we study the heroes of Scripture we clearly see this pattern. When God gives a promise, there are obstacles that need to be overcome before the promises are achieved and the seed grows into a promised tree that bears fruit.

The promise is like a dream that God plants within us. The dream that we have in the night that gives us vision. The purpose we see a bit far off, but believe in. The promise is there so that we have something big and beautiful to hold on to. Ultimately, the seed of promise, if we hold on and believe it, gives us energy to overcome the obstacles that are almost certainly going to come our way.

We see this pattern in three inspiring mothers from Scripture: Jochebed the mother of Moses, Hannah the mother of Samuel, and Mary the mother of Jesus.

First they received a promise. A seed that plants unfathomable hope inside of them. It's not merely human hope, but supernatural hope from the Father. And almost the very next moment, they encounter one or more seemingly insurmountable obstacles. They will have to persevere greatly to overcome them.

Does it sound familiar in your own life? Promise received. Why is it not easily realized, especially if it truly is from the Father? I'm just telling you what Scripture teaches us. We repeatedly witness resistance, therefore growth and perseverance are required before promises are able to become anything of substance.

What we see in the Biblical pattern is that our heroes (and it applies directly to us) ultimately achieve and receive only a portion of their promised inheritance. This is a difficult truth that many of us prefer not to dwell on. But to be true to God's word we have to take a closer look. The promise is only partially fulfilled in their lifetime.

Spoiler alert for what comes next, and this part is good news: by God the Father's grace, a huge part of the promise *is* fulfilled.

As we mine for treasures from their journeys of faith, I believe that the Holy Spirit wants each of us to revisit the promises spoken over our own lives. It is also a possibility that you haven't heard a promise yet for your life. Or perhaps you've lost sight of what your promise is.

What harm could there be in leaning in to hear and also receive new promises from God today? Consider the first mother I mentioned.

Jochebed was the mother of Moses. I don't think she gets as much credit as she deserves, at least not from the average Bible reader or pulpit. When you think about her life, she lived at a time when the most priceless promise Yahweh had given, was that a deliverer was going to rise up to save Israel from their centuries-long slavery in Egypt.

A deliverer was promised to finally break Jochebed and her people free from oppression. But then came the obstacle. As soon as this promise was prophesied, Pharaoh (the antichrist spirit of his day) proclaimed a new decree: wipe out all of the baby boys born to the Hebrews. Start now, and don't stop until I say so.

From the moment of the promise, every Israelite was forced to reconcile the irony. Their deliverance coincided with their loss and unbearable sorrow. Every newborn boy was to be cast naked into the Nile river. *Every son*.

The promise of a deliverer was held dearly by the Israelites. Living in slavery, their only hope came from Scripture as they clung to every word of prophecy for a better tomorrow. They knew there was a deliverer coming but Pharaoh believed that left unchecked, at the rate of their increase within the slave camps, the Israelites would become so powerful that they would overthrow Egypt, the great empire of that era. The sons of Israel would overwhelm and dominate, so he thought, the sons of Egypt.

According to a census in the Book of Numbers their were 2 million able-bodied fighting men when Israel arrived at Mt. Sinai only a generation later. If they had the will and the military leader, Israel may legitimately have had the power to overthrow the tyrant of their day. And so Pharaoh's promise-testing decree went out, to wipe out the baby boom before Israel could realize his own strength.

Perhaps the wildest part of the story, is how the baby boom and Pharaoh's genocide overlapped with the birth of the child of promise. Jochebed delivered Moses and Moses was called to deliver her people. When she saw him, she declared, "this is no ordinary child."

But Pharaoh's decree had gone out. Every living boy was to be drowned, cast naked into the Nile. If you haven't done the math, the arrival of a male deliverer is mathematically impossible if every single boy is put to death.

The Levite daughter of a priest, Jochebed was also married to a priest. She made a decision based on two impossible options: flee to a far away land and become a refugee, most likely dying during her personal exodus, or trust the promise of God the Father and hide him, somehow, within the pagan nation of Egypt. She heard other mothers and fathers screaming when their children were stolen away. Did she stay up all night, every night, afraid that the soldiers might steal her son, and kill him too, all the while trying to muffle her newborn baby's screams?

Baby Moses, like every baby, was completely dependent on his mother. Even the greatest emperor, warrior or champion arrives in that same posture of surrender. There is nothing a baby can do on its own.

My own son, Judah, is not yet two years old. He can rarely be left alone for more than 30 seconds at this stage of his life. Now that he's mobile, and not too aware of his body or oversized head weight, left alone he can easily fall down the stairs, tumble over a shoestring, burn himself on our fireplace or get into any number of things that he shouldn't get into.

Not only was Moses helpless, but there was a tyrannical regime trying to wipe the children of Israel off the face of the earth.

Perhaps Jochebed had a vision or a dream. Maybe a prompting or message that allowed her to do something as crazy as what she did next. As a mother, if you're reading this, imagine yourself in Jochebed's thought process when she made this decision. All her emotions were raging faster than the Nile as she considered the possibility of losing her precious baby. She then made, fashioned, formed, a basket. She wove her basket from the hyssop bush and put tar or sap over it, called pitch, to seal it from the elements. It would need to be waterproof.

What was on this mother's mind? I believe she was thinking about the way Yahweh had delivered her people before. She was raised as the daughter of a priest and knew the story well. The story of the ark that sustained Noah and his family during the flood.

While Jochebed's ark was built at a much smaller scale, her basket coated in pitch resembled Noah's ark in dramatic ways. It would prove no less miraculous a deliverance.

As a woman of deep faith, she put every shred of her belief into her basket. Imagine the care she took to weave it in the darkest hours of the night. Perhaps a solo candle burning at nine months pregnant. How she hid the baby bump is another mystery. But there she was, weaving and crafting and making the most beautiful offering of faith that you can possibly imagine. And more beautiful still was how her Father Yahweh would choose to receive her gift.

Faith can move mountains. Faith can silence waves. Faith is a miraculous and mysterious power that can spontaneously produce a breakthrough. Why? Because true faith is only carried by children who know *who* their Father is. And true faith moves the Father's heart.

Jochebed offered up a faith that was precious. Her hope was aflame like that solo candle, at times flickering, but always believing and releasing a radiant light, even in the dark corners of Egypt. She knit her basket together and coated it in the same pitch her forefathers used to waterproof the ark. Perhaps her last move was based on an idea from

God the Father Himself. In the end, ironically, she obeyed Pharaoh's order to throw her male baby into the raging Nile.

The Nile was no smooth-flowing tributary, it was the main artery and perhaps the only fresh water source flowing through Egypt. Water is life and water in the desert is abundant life. There are also dangerous, wild animals, in the Nile. When my brothers and I were in Kenya in 2006 we noted when we went to Lake Victoria that there were no swimmers in the water. None. It was a beautiful, hot day and absolutely nobody was going in the water. We learned that hippopotamuses kill more people than any other animal in Africa. They can completely submerge until swimmers have no idea they are there, and when they attack a person their jaws are swift and powerful enough to sever a person in half. With one bite.

Jochebed placed her fragile baby into a basket in the rushing water of the Nile. And Scripture tells us that her basket was found by the daughter of Pharaoh. The daughter of the same villain responsible for wiping out a generation of Israelites would become the father figure for Moses.

How much more twisted a plot can you get? It's the plot twist in the movie that is so ridiculous you struggle to believe it. The absentee, abusive, violent, murderous father ends up being the guy who takes in the future deliverer of the Israelite people. It's also an incredibly hard person, if not the most preposterous choice a mother could imagine, to have in authority over your son. But Jochebed knew there was a promise from God. A deliverer was going to rise up. She also believed that there was something about her baby, Moses, that set him apart.

Exodus 2:2 - *she saw he was a fine child.*

Another translation says she saw he was no ordinary child. In the Hebrew when it uses that statement it means that the face of the child glowed like an angel! When Moses was born he was so anointed by the Holy Spirit, he had such a calling on his life, that his face glowed like an angel of God! This proved to be one of the great testimonies of his life, a story and testimony that would follow him from glory to glory throughout his abundant life. Even Paul the apostle pointed out the glowing, the glory, on Moses' face when he descended the mountain. His face was alight because Moses saw his Father, Yahweh, face to face. Moses became a son.

Jochebed believed if she gave up the care of her baby as an offering to the Lord then her Father in Heaven could find a home and find a mother and even a father to care for him. When we get a promise, like she did, and choose to grab hold of it, we become bearers of the most valuable resource on either side of Heaven: Faith. And along with it, we will encounter obstacles.

What baskets have you been weaving together in faith?

For the mother of Moses, the promise was the future deliverance of her people. The obstacles were obvious: first of all, he probably would not even survive the initial stage of the plan. That is, the river float. But even after he did survive, the fulfilment of Jochebed's promise took a generation!

Was Jochebed still alive when Israel entered the promised land? Almost surely not. Did she get to go with, and see her people leave the land of slavery and pursue their promised land? Possibly. Did She live to see her other son and daughter, Aaron and Miriam, both become pivotal leaders in the move of God that finally brought true freedom to Israel? I believe that she did.

A portion of the promise she saw fulfilled, was that her son became great. Her son became a prince of Pharaoh. Her son became an important and powerful leader in the greatest nation on earth at that time. Her son grew to lead the greatest movement of refugees in history, pioneering a migration away from tyranny that would be spoken of through the ages.

There's such an interesting relationship between Israel and Egypt. Egypt was the ruling empire for centuries, perhaps most dominant during the lifetime of Moses. Yet, by a sovereign work of Yahweh, the Father, all throughout Israel's history an Israelite was often placed at the right hand of the Egyptian king. Shockingly, Moses was placed at the right hand of Pharaoh. But he wasn't the first Hebrew to have that honor.

Earlier, Moses' forefather Joseph became the second in command of Pharaoh in that same nation. And if you read the story of Esther it happened *again* when Mordecai, a Jew (and Esther's uncle), was placed at the right hand of the king of the most powerful nation on earth. Even as a foreigner he was elevated to the second in command in their nation!

What is God the Father doing? Something similar happens in the Book of Daniel when that Jewish prophet was exiled into Babylon to rise to Nebuchadnezzar's second in command. Not only a foreigner, but essentially a slave, and he too gained similar status. Just like Moses.

The Father is painting a picture for us of SONSHIP. He's revealing that as a good Father, he wants His own chosen sons to rule and to reign. He wants them to rule with the right kind of authority and wisdom. He wants them to reveal, even to pagans, or perhaps especially to pagans, that there is a true Father and King in Heaven, seeking the lost sons and daughters of this world.

The Father will go to almost any length imaginable to place His sons in rulership, because everyone benefits when the sons of the Father are in positions of authority.

When there is a promise from God in a person's life, God will bring what seems impossible in our human understanding, to fulfilment. Jochebed indeed saw at least some fulfilment of the promise. Her son became a prince rather than receive his death sentence 40 years earlier. But it was another 40 years of wandering in the desert for Moses before he returned to fulfill the promise completely, by delivering his mother's people.

To see the complete fulfilment of her promise, Jochebed would need to have lived one hundred to one hundred twenty years by the time of the exodus. Perhaps the author of the book would have noted her pilgrimage in the Scripture when the exodus of Israel took place, but perhaps not. For the sake of reasonable doubt, let's just imagine that she was not part of the nation that walked away from the oppression and slavery of Egypt.

Even still, Jochebed saw much of the promise from God fulfilled in her own lifetime. As she closed her eyes and went to her Heavenly Father, she left the earth as a legendary mother among mothers. She died not merely believing, but knowing that her son was the promised deliverer of her people. And therefore the child that she delivered by faith, indeed, delivered many.

Another mother who contributes to the mosaic of Biblical sonship is Hannah, the mother of Samuel. Hannah's faith inspires me. And her heartfelt cry to our Father in Heaven, moved Him so powerfully, that He responded to her faith by giving her one of Israel's most legendary prophets.

Hannah's life is a testimony that faith triumphs over the pain we face or have to endure through different seasons in our lives. She desired to bear children, and she believed that a seed of promise was planted within her. She believed one day she would see offspring.

But she was barren.

Barrenness is a relatively common theme in the story of women called to be godly mothers, not only in Scripture, but also in many families today. There are women who desire so deeply to bring life into the world. But they are unable to bear children.

Similarly, after dreaming about the promise of having her own child, a terrifying obstacle emerged - Hannah remained unable to conceive. For many years. Hannah faced the ultimate enemy of fruitfulness. Barrenness.

Take note of her journey, because it resembles almost every single story in the bloodline of the human lineage of Jesus Christ, the Messiah. At some point in many of the patriarch's stories, after receiving their promise, Hannah's ancestors encountered barrenness too. The promise was clear: "You will have offspring." The promise was to bring life into the world. Some of Hannah's forefathers were brought up with incredible, over the top promises, only to encounter what looked like insurmountable obstacles.

Abraham and Sarah were told they would have descendants as numerous as the sand on the seashore and the stars in the sky. But as time went on, Sarah reached 90 years old, and she had still not borne even one child in her old age.

It's a pretty major hurdle to the promise of countless descendants! Enter Hannah, a daughter of Sarah in the passage of generations, and a true fulfilment of those promised stars and grains of sand. She went faithfully to the temple and she believed, she truly believed in Yahweh, her Heavenly Father. She loved her husband, she was a faithful leader in her community, she was penitent before God.

One day, at the temple, Hannah was weeping on account of her painful lack, a void that existed in her womb, despite her faith. Beyond her primary obstacle of barrenness, her husband also had another wife. The second wife (in what was undoubtedly a bizarre love triangle) had the audacity, like Leah before her, to mock Hannah for being unable to bear children. Salt in the deepest of open wounds. You'll find a similar account in the story of Rachel in Genesis 29.

And the saddest part, was that the other wife knew the joy of bearing children. In her jealousy for their husband's love, she lorded her motherhood over Hannah, bringing a painful sting to the already tormenting sorrow within Hannah's soul. Along with jealousy, hers was a home filled with grief and shame.

As she suffered, Hannah's pain grew to uncontrollable weeping outside the tabernacle in Shiloh, and her display caught the attention of the high priest Eli. Rather than have pity on her at first, he thought she was drunk! Eli was probably not a discerning priest, based on that response and the story of his parentage of Hophni and Phineas, his rebellions and sinful sons. When Hannah was beside herself with sorrow, crying out bitterly before the Lord, her high priest was unable to respond like a true father. Eli simply assumed she was out of her mind.

But Yahweh still worked through Eli, despite his lack of insight in Hannah's darkest hour. After Hannah described her grief, and her plan to dedicate her child into the service of the temple, Eli ultimately had compassion on her. He prophesied to her that her prayer would be answered. That when she returned next year, she would not be returning empty handed.

She was going to have a son. A new seed of promise was planted in her barren soul. And the fulfilment of her promise would bring blessing to all the sons of Israel.

Incredibly, only weeks later, Hannah became pregnant. The very next year she had a baby, and with a joy that only a mother can truly know, she named her son Samuel, meaning, "God has heard."

1 Samuel 3:1 *The boy Samuel served the Lord under Eli. In those days the Lord did not speak directly to people very often; there were very few visions.*

From the womb of a barren woman, came forth a prophet so great, that not one, not two, but at least three books in the Bible have been credited to his authorship. A prophet so great, that in a time when people were not commonly hearing from the Lord or receiving visions from the Holy Spirit, the audible voice of Father God arrived as a life-altering whisper in Samuel's pre-teenage ear. A boy, who even as a man, knew what it meant to be a son of the Father.

We live in a time of great blessing. In Samuel and Hannah's day, they did not have what we have. They did not have the Holy Spirit available to all who received salvation. That gift was destined to be given centuries later at Pentecost. But God the Father was pleased to choose a son in Samuel, from a barren woman, to become the great prophet of his generation.

And this leads to one of the key reasons why Hannah's story, and the life of Samuel are not only the fulfilment of a beautiful promise, but also a key revelation for us about sonship.

Sons of the Father hear the Father's voice. Sons of the father know His intimate whisper. Sons of the Father share the thoughts that originate from the very heart of God, with a hungry, thirsty and desperate world. May we, like Hannah and Samuel, learn to hear and treasure our Father's voice.

Hannah's miracle son, Samuel, quickly grew into a priest before the Lord who commonly heard the Father's voice. The voice that even the high priest Eli was unable to hear. Consider this: when God spoke, Eli the high priest was unable to recognize the Father. It took several repetitions to get his attention.

But then again, even for high priests, the voice of Father God was *rare* in those days.

I wonder how jealous Eli was to hear God's precious voice again. His own soul longing to experience the presence and comfort of the Most High. Did Eli feel the same jealousy of Peninnah, Elkanah's other wife, and bitterly scorn the young prodigy at first? Did he plead with Yahweh to speak once again to his aged, but hungry soul?

God chose to confide in Samuel instead of the high priest, Eli. Samuel, a boy with clean hands and a pure heart. There was something about his mother's dedication that raised the bar for Samuel's life. There was something about her perseverance, how she overcame the obstacles in her own story. How she chose to relinquish her greatest desire, a son, and dedicate him to the Lord. Could Samuel have possibly been so special, if not for his beloved mother? And so we see in Hannah, that our mothers play an essential role in developing their children towards maturity on the path to sonship.

Hannah prayed, "I will give this child of promise back to you, Father." She was willing to relinquish her greatest gift, if only it were received in love by her great King. Even though Hannah could have raised a king in her own house, she was willing to give up her precious, one and only son. Does her parental love and sacrifice sound at all familiar? She wanted to receive the one promise that was better. Hannah saw an even greater promise further off. She longed to see future generations partake in the Father's inheritance.

Not as slaves and not as orphans, but as sons.

If she doubted at the tabernacle, or on the long journey home from Shiloh, Hannah knew God's promises and kingdom were real when she received Samuel's miraculous life. She grew to full term and screamed with delight as Samuel entered the world. She held the promise in her hands and coddled him with unreserved love. She sang lullabies that astounded angels and her praises ascended to the very throne of God.

Here, she decided, was an offering worthy to be placed at the feet of the Father. "Father, God of Angel Armies, I give you full rights to my son." We can learn a lot from the simple prayer of Hannah's heart. A prayer that activated her sacrifice, while releasing generational blessings.

From my human reading of the story, Hannah's greatest obstacle was yet to be overcome. Now that she actually held her baby boy, would she be willing to give her son into full time service in the Lord's tabernacle? To give her long-awaited baby up, after weaning him. In the Middle East, the age of weaning was between 3 to 5 years old. As just a kindergarten-aged boy, she dedicated Samuel into the priest's service - full time.

We understand, by seeing the entire story in one reading, that Samuel became one of the greatest prophets in the history of the world. But Hannah had to walk out all those long years in trust. Her hope would have otherwise been dashed almost as suddenly as it arrived.

Later, Hannah saw the fulfilment of the promise when she heard tell of the new king of Israel's anointing. The age of the judges ended with her son. Her son, Samuel, walked by all of Jesse's stronger and more handsome sons to anoint David as the incoming King of Israel. The king whose throne Jesus Himself would choose to sit upon. It was Samuel who recognized that king. When David was merely a boy, Samuel anointed him. Crowned him with Heaven's blessing. Declared that he would be the leader of God's people Israel.

Perhaps his moment in the quiet resonated most loudly in that moment, when looking upon a teenager in David, Samuel flashed back to those years long ago in the tabernacle, when the voice of Yahweh rang so loud and clear to his teenage ear. In Samuel's memory, a young David was not only a real possibility for the Father to work with, but likely the better choice. Pure, unblemished, unbelievably humble. A son that could serve well enough to be called a king.

Samuel went through his primary calling and training as a child, too. He was able to recognize the signs of calling and training in young David. More than that, Samuel heeded his Father's voice, knowing that while man sees the outer things, Yahweh perceives the condition of one's heart. And if the Father spoke, Samuel listened.

But the promise of fruitfulness did not end for Hannah with Samuel. She received five more children after him. Five is a picture not only of fruitfulness and abundance, but Biblically represents grace. There was grace on Hannah's life because she followed through. She was willing to see a greater destiny for her people and her relatives and partake in a future inheritance that surpassed anything she could possibly receive in this life.

Hannah serves as an example of the benefits we achieve by sacrificing for a short time, in order to receive something much greater in the coming Kingdom.

Another Biblical mother who teaches us a great deal about sonship is the woman who became the mother of the Son of God Himself.

One of my favourite moments in the entire Bible, is the story of Gabriel visiting Mary. There's one thing about the story that I can't seem to shake lately: God sent one of the greatest beings in the universe to deliver the message. Obviously that was for a reason. The good news he carried was like no message ever delivered, or ever to be delivered again. Gabriel, the fiercely powerful archangel. In fact, Gabriel is one of only four angels named, who serve full-time before the Father's throne in Heaven.

Imagine this: Gabriel lives in the throne room of Yahweh. He probably rarely, if ever, leaves his post. But if an occasion is big enough, if an announcement from Father God's throne can not be mishandled, on the rarest of occasions, Gabriel is chosen to deliver a message to humanity. He made a personal visit to Mary in the opening of the New covenant story of the promised Messiah.

Angels are described throughout the Bible as messengers. They specialize in doing the bidding of the Father. But they are also described as messengers and servants on behalf of another party: humanity.

Angels, by definition and design, were created to work on behalf of the sons and daughters of the King. Those with a full revelation of sonship recognize their authority, and access, even to angels.

Our authority as sons is so precious to God, that the Father created divine beings, angels, to operate a type of heavenly delivery service. Think of it this way: do you need to place an order for provision, do you need a miracle, or have any request from your Heavenly Father? He will even send angels to fulfill the needs of his sons and daughters.

To serve and partner and act as messengers on behalf of God to humanity, is a primary function of the angelic realm. But there are even more powerful angels within the heavenly realm than the many angels at work in the world today. A choice few have unique roles and serve permanently before Almighty God in the actual presence of the Father. And Gabriel, an angel who even non-believers know by name, was the angel sent by Yahweh to announce the greatest story ever told to Mary for the very first time.

Let's not take the moment for granted just because we've heard it before or seen it (perhaps poorly) portrayed in any number of Christmas pageants. It was a big promise. A promise that blew the mind of the most revered mother in history. Try to imagine your reaction if you had been Mary at the center-frame of this famous Scripture.

Luke 1: 26-38 The Birth of Jesus Foretold

In the sixth month of Elizabeth's pregnancy, God sent the angel Gabriel to Nazareth, a town in Galilee, to a virgin pledged to be married to a man named Joseph, a descendant of David. The virgin's name was Mary. The angel went to her and said, "Greetings, you who are highly favored! The Lord is with you."

Mary was greatly troubled at his words and wondered what kind of greeting this might be. But the angel said to her, "Do not be afraid, Mary; you have found favor with God. You will conceive and give birth to a son, and you are to call him Jesus. He will be great and will be called the Son of the Most High. The Lord God will give him the throne of his father David, and he will reign over Jacob's descendants forever; his kingdom will never end."

"How will this be," Mary asked the angel, "since I am a virgin?"

The angel answered, "The Holy Spirit will come on you, and the power of the Most High will overshadow you. So the holy one to be born will be called the Son of God. Even Elizabeth your relative is going to have a child in her old age, and she who was said to be unable to conceive is in her sixth month. For no word from God will ever fail."

"I am the Lord's servant," Mary answered. "May your word to me be fulfilled." Then the angel left her.

Her jaw had to be on the floor. The most profound, gut-wrenching mic drop in history began with a phrase that proves beyond a shadow of a doubt that Mary was anointed for sonship. Sons receive the promises given to them by their Father. Even if a promise is all but impossible to believe.

How can Mary understand sonship as a woman? As discussed previously, sonship transcends gender. We can turn to Galatians 3:28 for a quick explanation from Scripture: "There is neither Jew nor Gentile, neither slave nor free, nor is there male and female, for you are all one in Christ Jesus."

Catch this! We are all ONE in Christ Jesus.

Here's a sad but necessary pause to reflect on modern society! The enemy only knows how to counterfeit. If the enemy were a drug dealer, he would never pay in real currency. It would always be a fake.

There is a war going on right now in our time, yes, you and I are in the middle of the battlefield. The war is not yet over. It may take on different nuance, but it rages on. One of the battlefields where the enemy loves to wage war, is over the prevailing culture and status quo of society.

Gender identity has become a massive battleground in the world and a threat to many believers, particularly to anyone not on guard or aware of the devil's schemes. Thankfully, there is a simple answer to the crazy battle going on: Satan, the old snake from the Garden, is a deceiver. He works to shortcut the plans of God in order to deceive anyone who he can lead into temptation. Paul the apostle described the followers of Satan as those who go after shameful lusts with a constant desire for more.

The Devil says we are neither male nor female, but can be any or both genders plus another hundred or more new genders only recently defined. The Father says we are neither male nor female, but ONE in Christ Jesus.

Can you see the counterfeit in the enemy's version? It's a lie spun off a Biblical truth. It's an inversion. Look for the simple and basic methods the enemy uses in every area of culture today. You'll realize very quickly that Satan has no creativity!

The Creator of everything, our Heavenly Father, is the creative one. And His sons (again this label also applies to His daughters) are creative too. What a truth to believe for your own life: *you are creative*, and even the Devil and his angels are not!

Can you see why the jealousy of the enemy rages like an unquenchable fire against the children of God? The Father's sons are outdoing divine beings on a regular basis. You are in that

company…if you know that you are a son of the Father.

Back to Mary. Her promise arrives. It's delivered by one of the four most powerful angels in the entire universe. Now I understand why Mary was afraid when Gabriel entered the room. The promise, upon first hearing, was so ridiculous you could scarcely imagine any human believing it. Father God planned to use teenage Mary as the miraculous conduit of salvation for humanity. Miraculously, supernaturally, to do something that had never been done in the history of the world.

I don't really want to get too far off base here, but there is one more counterfeit that Gabriel's message to Mary reveals. There were divine beings, ironically they were angels who Scripture refers to as 'sons of God.' They were beings from ages past who rebelled against Father God and left their heavenly domain.

Their offspring were called Nephilim, the giants that we meet in Genesis 6, in the early days of humanity. But the divine sons who left Heaven were trying to achieve an early counterfeit of the eventual fulfilment that came through Mary! Can you see it?

Genesis 6:1 explains, *"When man began to multiply on the face of the land and daughters were born to them, the sons of God saw that the daughters of man were attractive. And they took as their wives any they chose."*

This is beyond a Stephen King novel or any far-out science fiction plot from a twisted, modern movie. Actually this is the kind of history that inspires such writings: there is a group of divine beings who left Heaven, to take for themselves wives, corrupting their immortal bodies, in exchange for creating a hybrid offspring that was partly human and partly divine.

What in the actual world?!

Does it sound a bit like Greek mythology? That's where these archetypes come from. The stories passed down become legend. Or as Galadriel so aptly put it in the prologue of the Lord of the Rings trilogy, "History became legend. Legend became myth."

The enemy tried, in those days, to not only counterfeit the plan of Father God. He tried to render the plan of Yahweh impossible. By making all human blood corrupt. Angels and women made offspring together. The enemy was working to tarnish the image of God, in essence, by polluting the earth with transgression. It was a divine counterfeit that failed.

The Father has better plans. The Father is too creative to be stopped by any amount of scheming or debauchery.

The Father, before time began at the first sunrise, had already established Salvation as the ultimate divine strategy for victory. He had already witnessed the sacrifice of His own Son before the creation of the world. It would be through the promised seed, through Mary being overshadowed by the Holy Spirit, that humble Mary would produce the ONE Heavenly Man, Jesus Christ. She would be a mother unlike any other.

Jesus was indeed one of a kind, like no-one before or after Him. But we can't miss the mother of all mothers in His story, because she only birthed the Son of God because she was a son of the Father!

Jesus was born of the virgin Mary, who believed in her impossible promise. And if you want to talk about obstacles, Mary faced them. Rejection from her conservative synagogue, check. Rejection from any friends or family who didn't believe in virgin conception (which had never once happened in history), check. Rejection for at least a time from her betrothed Joseph, until he was told by God in a dream to marry her, because she told no lie, check.

The unseen realm was shaken by the news: Mary was pregnant by the Holy Spirit. And in her womb, Mary carried the one true Son of the Father. The firstborn among many brothers. The Heavenly Man, Jesus Christ.

I long to enter the time warp of history as a fly on the wall inside Mary and Joseph's nursery room. The secret ponderings of Mary's heart coming alive through lullabies and prayers and tears shed for joy that among the billions ever created, she alone would be called, "Mother of Messiah."

She treasured up gold and wealth immeasurable in her precious soul. For when she kissed her little baby, she did indeed kiss the face of God.

We see this same pattern in the lives of Jochebed, Hannah and Mary. They all became legends and matriarchs in history.

First, the promise came, and they believed the promise was for them. Next, they encountered resistance. Obstacles, trauma or challenges that attempted to roadblock their destiny. And in the end, all three saw at least partial fulfilment in their promises.

They experienced God's faithfulness and lived to see an inheritance within their lifetime. Most of all, they passed along a blessing to future generations, by empowering their sons to walk faithfully, so that their sons passed immeasurable generational blessings to their own physical and spiritual offspring.

CHAPTER SEVEN
THREE RULES OF SONSHIP

Studying the life of Jesus as God's Son, I have found at least three keys to walking in sonship in our daily lives. The first one is to simply behold Him.

First, we are invited to "Look to the Son."

John the Baptist was called the greatest prophet in history because He identified who the Son of God was. There were many that came and went, some people thought prophets like Elijah were the Son of God, or that anointed men like King David or John the Baptist were the Messiah.

But John himself looked and said in John 1:29, *"Behold the Lamb of God who takes away the sins of the world."* He looked to the Son and saw new life.

John 5:11-12
And this is the testimony: God has given us eternal life, and this life is in his Son. Whoever has the Son has life; whoever does not have the Son of God does not have life.

When we look to the Son, we have life. Thankfully we don't have to be the greatest prophet on earth to recognize Jesus today. He has already been revealed to us. We just have to look to the Son. When we look we behold that He alone takes away our sins. He alone makes us new.

Second, you must "Receive your identity from the Father."

Another key to walking in sonship in your daily life is to receive your identity from the Father. Do not accept any other identity besides the one God your Father gives to you. Imagine what the world would look like if every single saved believer walked around with a daily consciousness of their right relationship to Yahweh! It would literally be heaven on earth. Every work of the enemy would be destroyed by these fiercely anointed children of God.

Matthew 3:13-17
Then Jesus came from Galilee to the Jordan to be baptized by John. But John tried to deter him, saying, "I need to be baptized by you, and do you come to me?" Jesus replied, "Let it be so now; it is proper for us to do this to fulfill all righteousness." Then John consented. As soon as Jesus was baptized, he went up out of the water. At that moment heaven was opened, and he saw the Spirit of God descending like a dove and alighting on him.

And a voice from heaven said, "This is my Son, whom I love; with him I am well pleased."

The beginning of Jesus Christ's ministry was marked by two incredibly significant moments.

First, He was called "the beloved Son of God." The Heavenly Father audibly spoke to a massive crowd, pointing out clearly, for the first time in Jesus' life, that the man standing before them was in fact His Son. It's important to continue reading to see what God said next. Because after specifying their relationship, God went a step further and declared, "with Him I am well pleased."

God the Father used similar verbiage to the moment when he made Adam and Eve. He was pleased with his son and daughter and said, "they are very good." Similarly, He showed pleasure in His beloved Son, Yahshua, or Jesus.

Identity is the foundation of everything we say and do. What we believe about who we are is reflected in our lives every single day. Subtly or overtly, our identity guides everything. It rudders the ship. It's the steering wheel inside the car.

This declaration by His Father rooted Christ in His true identity and set the stage for everything that came next. It pointed Jesus to true North for the rest of His ministry on Earth. He later shared His own revelation of this truth in the Book of John, with one of my favourite truths in the entire Scripture.

In John 10:30 Jesus declared, *"I and my Father are one."*

Just pause there for a moment. Jesus is called the Son of God by His Father. We know that He was conceived of the Holy Spirit and was no ordinary man. But he's also the model that we look to for sonship.

Jesus says, "I and my Father are one." So His identification with Yahweh the Father reveals that He is *in Yahweh* and *Yahweh is in Him*.

So often in humanity, we hear about sons resembling their fathers. The way a man carries himself, physically resembles his father. They may look the same, walk the same, share idiosyncrasies or other character traits.

Consider careers and lifestyle choices. In essentially every generation of humanity until some point in the 1900's, basically for all of human history until the last few decades, the son took on the career or trade of his father. If you had a father who was a carpenter, you grew up knowing you were going to be a carpenter. Joseph, the earthly father of Jesus was a carpenter, so that was the trade Jesus carried on. When Joseph died, Jesus inherited the family business before beginning a short season of active ministry.

There's an embedding of this truth within Judaism, and generally within non-Western cultures to such a degree, that it is understood that whatever a person does, whoever they become, has been handed down by their fathers.

You'll see a line come up in many stories in the Scriptures, 'Our forefathers did this.' It's understood that because their fathers did something, they are bound to doing it too.

This includes the good, the bad and the ugly. If children saw their parents worshiping idols, they grew up worshiping idols. If their fathers visited the shrine prostitutes, they visited shrine prostitutes. Following a forefather can be a very bad thing.

That's another reason why Jesus' arrival as the Son of the Father was so important. The broken ways of men were ultimately inverted when Jesus unveiled how a true son is supposed to reflect the Father.

Even when He arrived on the scene as a twelve year old boy, wowing the scholars in the temple, Jesus stated that He must be, "going about His Father's business." What was this child talking about? His father, Joseph, was a carpenter. Hearing Jesus' words they reasoned that Jesus would someday become a craftsman like His father Joseph. Honouring His earthly father and following the pattern of His culture, Jesus did become a carpenter.

But Jesus actually meant that His Father was Yahweh, The Creator of everything, the Heavenly Father and God Most High. So when Jesus talked about doing the Father's business, He was unveiling a brand new meaning for the phrase. His Father was in the business of cleansing lepers, healing the sick, casting out demons, raising the dead, breaking off yokes of oppression, freeing the captives, bringing liberty in place of bondage, and giving away peace, life and authority to humanity. Jesus was concerned with whatever affairs His Father was concerned with. After all, it was His job as a Son to carry on the family business.

And rather than doing backflips and setting off an instant revival that would have swept the Earth, when Jesus revealed to the religious leaders that He was in fact Yahweh's Son, they picked up stones to stone him. Israel, called to be God's own inheritance and actually labeled the sons of God after they were established as God's chosen people, did not collectively respond to the call to actually *be* His sons.

Thankfully, the great apostles and early disciples became sons. They serve as examples for us to this day. As true children, they were among the elect few who faithfully followed their Father.

Now you and I are invited to pick up where Jesus and his followers left off, and carry on the Father's business. If we become sons of the Father, we live as heirs of the fullness of God.

With His last words on earth, Jesus prayed in John 17:20-26, *"I am not asking on behalf of my disciples alone, but also on behalf of those who will believe in Me through their message, that all of them may be one, as You, Father, are in Me, and I am in You. May they also be in Us, so that the world may believe that You sent Me. I have given them the glory You gave Me, so that they may be one as We are one— I in them and You in Me—that they may be perfectly united, so that the world may know that You sent Me and have loved them just as You have loved Me. Father, I want those You have given Me to be with Me where I am, that they may see the glory You gave Me because You loved Me before the foundation of the world. Righteous Father, although the world has not known You, I know You, and they know that You sent Me. And I have made Your name known to them and will continue to make it known, so that the love You have for Me may be in them, and I in them."*

I want to highlight how important this is for us right now on earth. These were the last recorded prayers of Christ. Literally minutes later, Judas pointed out Jesus to the Roman soldiers who arrested Him. He was then given a false trial and ultimately, crucified.

In the last moments of His life on earth, Jesus spent His time praying for you and for me. And not only that, but he prayed that you and I would have a revelation of what it means to be a son of God, like He was.

Jesus could have prayed anything, but His prayer was that we would identify as sons of the Father.

Finally, to walk in sonship you have to receive the Holy Spirit.

The Spirit is the living Breath empowering you to actually *live* as a son, and not depend upon your own strength or ability.

At the baptism of Jesus, after being identified as God the Father's beloved Son, the Holy Spirit rested and dwelt upon and began operating from inside of Jesus. Like Him, we need to receive the Holy Spirit.

Have you experienced this life-altering moment yet in your own life?

If it has taken place, you will know that it has. The first step is looking to the Son, and allowing Father God to speak over your identity. If you accept His calling, you will let Father God claim you as His child. You will never receive the Holy Spirit if you skip that step. I don't believe that you can receive the Holy Spirit until your true identity has been revealed to, or spoken over you.

We've all seen people in our lives who are stuck. Sometimes we get frustrated, because the very nature of being stuck means that there are repeating behaviours or cycles that never seem to break. Regardless of one's effort, it can be impossible to snap out of the same old pattern.

Friends or family might even say something like, "That is now who you are." But at the very heart of any addiction or pattern of harm or sin, you will always find an identity issue.

Each child of God needs a new revelation of their identity as a son of the Father.

To keep such an important revelation operating in daily life, influencing your personal routines and decisions, you need a revelation of the consistent, working breath that Holy Spirit desires to breathe inside of you.

I believe without any doubt, that there is no gift as precious as the Holy Spirit! And despite being costly and precious, it is a free gift!

But before you receive this priceless gift, you have to be called out. You have to be told that you are a child of God, or need a breakthrough of belief in the value of your identity to God the Father, in order to receive this gift. When God the Father makes the identity claim of 'son' over you, you have to actually accept that you are His son.

That is the moment that qualifies you to receive God the Father's Holy Breath, the Holy Spirit of God. As God's son, you become more like Jesus every single day, because you become a bearer of the same Spirit that Jesus walked with in His own personal relationship with the Father.

And this is where it gets especially real in your life. At the time you receive the Holy Spirit of God, you will be empowered to do what the Father says to do. You will start being an owner and operator of the family business. Jesus told His followers in John 5:19, *"Very truly I tell you, the Son can do nothing by Himself; He can do only what He sees His Father doing, because whatever the Father does the Son also does."*

I personally find this to be very good news. As a son, none of us have to conjure anything up. Frankly, one of the reasons that I believe many Christians are afraid of the supernatural and actually afraid to learn about things like healing and miracles, is because they have experienced failure when they have tried to do things in and of themselves.

We have probably all done this at some point. You know what could be or would be a great move of God. So you feel like you are now responsible for making it happen. But if Jesus didn't work that way, why should we? Jesus only did what He saw the Father doing. He did what the Father revealed for Him to do. That is your business for the day: do what the Father shows you to do today.

Lean in and practice that. Lean in to hear His voice and sense His direction. Let the Holy Spirit (who is also the Father) take the wheel. Let the Holy Spirit lead you in your daily life, in your family activities, in your job responsibilities, in your actual life. The Good Shepherd wants to lead you.

And, He also *loves* when you respond to what He's saying and doing.

Romans 8:14

All those who are led by the Spirit of God, they are the sons of God.

I'm not saying that you will audibly hear the Father's voice regularly. That would be fantastic, but it's also not true in the experience of the saints or believers who I know. Many times, the prompting or impression that you are feeling *is* His voice. It could be a dream or a feeling you know in your gut. In the creative way that the Father speaks to you individually, He is telling you what to do or what move to make next.

But don't feel pressure when you hear His voice. You should feel a burden of responsibility (not a heavy burden that makes you feel overwhelmed) that is enough for you to take action. Remember that the saints and prophets of old were never unwilling to wait on the Father throughout this process.

Sometimes the clear direction comes after you take a small, initial step in the direction of what God is saying to do. Scripture is *filled with* times of waiting. As you pray and wait, life keeps happening. You can still eat and drink and work and worship and live your life in the times of waiting in your life.

Let the Father speak, and then do what He says to do. Follow through, but don't expect everything to take three seconds. Allow God your Father to work things out in your life. That is how you live like a son.

Follow His lead. And like a son, unafraid of your good Father, you also need to let, even invite, the Father to discipline you. Let Him walk things out with you.

Proverbs 3:12
Who Yahweh loves, he corrects; even as a father the son he delights in.

The Father is speaking over your identity. Turn off the noise and distractions, and hear what He has to say.

Look to Him.

Agree with His identity for you.

And receive the Holy Spirit.

I can not wait to see what happens as an army of sons of God grow more in tune with the Spirit's voice, and attend more consistently to the daily business matters of our Heavenly Father.

Living as sons, we will be walking in all the identity, all the inheritance and all the authority that Jesus walked in. And the other incredible thing is that we will go around bringing other lost souls into the Kingdom so that they can join the family business with us. The expansion of Yahweh's kingdom and power will dominate the workings and strategies of the enemy, and we will experience our Father's grace and goodness like we have never experienced it before.

Proverbs 10:1
A wise son brings joy to his father, but a foolish son grief to his mother.

Proverbs 23:24
The father of a righteous man will greatly rejoice, and he who fathers a wise son will delight in him.

CHAPTER EIGHT
THREE BENEFITS OF SONSHIP

There are more benefits to walking in sonship than I could possibly contain in one book. But there are three clear benefits I can point to, as an introduction, that we can mine from the pages of Scripture.

The first benefit of sonship is one I've seen time and again, from Canada to Africa, India to Colombia. Rich or poor, strong or weak, living or dead.

As a Son, your status is turned upside down.

A mystery of Heaven. The Creator of Heaven and Earth came to dwell among us. As one of us.

Emmanuel, God *with* us. Herod issued his decree to take the lives of all the children in the land, believing that the kingship of Jesus would supplant his rule and replace his power as political leader of the Jewish nation.

It's one of the things that never seems to go away: the perpetual power struggle in both the physical and spiritual realm, simultaneously. That ongoing battle kept Herod up at night too. It drove him mad. He had to be mad, and influenced by dark spirits, to take away all those precious babies' lives.

But there was one manifestation that Herod must have never considered. That the Savior of the world could possibly arrive as a king unrecognizable to human eyes. If Yahshua walked in to Herod's presence all those years later, Herod would not have believed that He was the Savior of the world even if someone told him. Which is why King Jesus gave him no response at all. Jesus was never interested in human politics.

Not only did Jesus *not* arrive as a king, dwelling in palaces or high places. But He lived on Earth as a homeless man. He ventured into the electrifying work of His Father's business, from the shameful town of Nazareth. A place so despised that the saying of the locals written on every bumper sticker and T-shirt was, "Nothing good ever comes out of Nazareth."

I've been listening to Rich Mullins a lot recently. He was a worship leader in the 90's, whose life was cut short when he died tragically in a car crash on the way to his own concert in 1997. But days before the accident he recorded an album called The Jesus Record, a temporary recording that was never going to be heard by anyone besides his own producer. It was a rough demo of new songs he would soon record in a fully equipped studio, with other professional musicians.

After he died, however, they released the EP alongside re-recordings of the songs by artists including Michael W Smith and Amy Grant. Then they posthumously released the album. Rich Mullins wrote the most amazing lyric on one of the tracks, and I can't seem to get his line out of my head:

The world can't stand what it can not own...and it can't own you, because you did not have a home. Birds have nests, foxes have dens, but the hope of the whole world rests on the shoulders of a homeless man ... because you did not have a home.

The creator of the very elements of Earth, the one Who designed the trees harvested to construct buildings, engineered the soil so it could be used to make bricks. The Creator of matter and energy and existence. He did not have a home.

Take heart if you are in a temporary dwelling yourself. Take heart if you are homeless or in need. Take heart if you are wondering if you can make your next bill payment or keep your vehicle running with one more gallon of fuel.

Christ's homelessness was not the result of a vow of poverty, or the product of bad choices, or caused by worldly rejection. Christ's poverty was a prophetic declaration that His Kingdom IS NOT OF THIS WORLD. The Kingdom of God and His Son can not be built by human hands.

Christ lived differently than Herod could have ever imagined a king might live. He did it to exemplify a powerful truth that we should take stock of today if we want to truly live as bearers of the Kingdom. If we truly want to live as sons of the Father.

Jesus was declaring, that you don't live IN the Kingdom. The Kingdom lives IN YOU.

The Father's Kingdom is one that turns the dweller into the dwelling place. It's a kingdom that is upside down.

In Jewish history, Moses was instructed to build a tabernacle, and then once purified and atoned for by ceremonies of cleansing, when all the sin and residue of this world were washed off, He could enter, while others stood far off, and only then could Moses come into Yahweh's dwelling place.

But it was a temporary dwelling place. Where He could only go for a short time, and even from within that intimate place, Moses still received from God, from a distance. But God Almighty's plan, our Heavenly Father's plan, was to live *in us*. You and I were always designed to become the royal palace, the divine dwelling, the castle of His presence!

In what surely is one of the most incredible Scriptures in the entire Bible, one that I've already pointed out, but deserves repeating due to it's importance regarding sonship. In Jesus' final prayer in the Garden of Gethsemane, He declared His ultimate desire, *"I pray also for those who will believe in me through their message, that all of them may be one, Father, just as you are in me and I am in you. May they also be in us so that the world may believe that you have sent me. I have given them the glory that you gave me, that they may be one as we are one— I in them and you in me—so that they may be brought to complete unity. Then the world will know that you sent me and have loved them even as you have loved me."*

Isaiah called Him, "God with us." That beautiful name, Emmanuel. And Here, Emmanuel Himself, prays that not only will He be with us but that He will dwell and live and reign *with-in* us, making us truly alive. Not only in the flesh, but in the Spirit. Alive for real.

One of my favourite promises in the Bible echoes this in Revelation 21:3 where it says, *"And then I heard a loud voice from the throne, saying, "See! The tabernacle of God is among men, and He will live among them, and they will be His people, and God Himself will be with them as their God."*

And so we learn that the status of an orphan turned into a son of the Father, is more powerful than the status of the world's greatest kings. There is another important point to be made about status in the

Father's house: Jesus repeatedly pointed out that the deeds of men that are done for status, out of selfish desire or hope for favour in this world, actually have no value at all.

In Matthew 20:16 Jesus said, *"So those who are last in this world shall be first in the world to come, and those who are first, last."*

Consider this thought today. Ponder it as you go about your tasks or put your head on the pillow. Consider it and meditate on it, and believe this when you encounter challenges that may even feel insurmountable in your life.

Even when you don't see things lining up on earth as you think they should, there is a future time where everything will be put into perfect, heavenly alignment.

If the Creator of Heaven lives inside of you, then you can be sure the fullness of the Father's Kingdom is about to be brought to bear in your life. If not now, then for eternity with Him.

A second benefit of sonship is that as God's son, time is for you, not against you.

This is mysterious, but it feels important to include in the benefits of sonship highlighted in this book.

Time is not moving in a straight line. I believe that someone reading this, (you may be young or you may be old), needs to hear this.

In Jewish circles, there is a weekly Scripture reading that correlates with their lunisolar calendar. Regardless of what may be taking place in the world, or outside a persons influence or control, Jews believe that the calendar and associated Scripture are what define the Jewish week. When they align with it, they are believing that God's opinion of the times will serve as the guide and reference point for the week's events, deeds and decisions.

A Rabbi named Rabbi Zalman calls this "living with the times." This has been a fascinating reality for me to experience in the last several years, and I believe that living with the times that God has put in place is not only possible, it's actually a calling on every disciple of Christ.

At specific moments, or in seasons throughout the last several years, I've felt prompted by God to look into certain dates and times in the Jewish calendar. And I have come to realize Yahweh has an upside down way with time that can bring reversals and changes so quickly and so specifically. When our good Father has set something to happen, it will unfold even when it makes no sense from a human perspective.

It even seems (at times) to go against the linear, factual, or even scientific reality of time.

Habakkuk prophesied this in Habakkuk 1:5 *[YAHWEH replied,] "Look among the nations! See! Be astonished! Wonder! For I am doing something in your days— You would not believe it if you were told - (even before it happens.)*

I shared with some people recently about the Hebrew year 5782. In Hebrew each number has a word and a picture associated with it. The 2, at the end of the year, is the word 'beht' in Hebrew and symbolizes a tent, dwelling place or a house.

Jesus did not have a home. He lived as a homeless man during His earthly ministry. Ironically, whereas Jesus had no place to lay his head, he wants us to be established and to have a dwelling place. One where he lives in us and we abide in Him, and we can be established to influence the earth - not using the worlds methods, but using the methods and weapons of His Kingdom.

These weapons include Love, Joy, Praise and Hope.

Messianic Christians and practicing Jews celebrate a festival every year called Shemini Atzeret. It's a pretty amazing day in the calendar, and most intriguingly it comes just after the feast of tabernacles. During that seven-day feast, the Jews were to set up a temporary dwelling, essentially a tent, to commemorate the tabernacle that Yahweh dwelt in while they were in the desert. It also served as a reminder of the fact that they were living in tents as wanderers in the wilderness.

Pause to think of the humility of God Almighty for a moment. His people are living in tents as nomads in the desert. So He enters a tent to move in with them! That is the Father and God of the Bible, a God of love and incredible relationship, Who operates in unfathomable loving kindness. And lives with His family as a Father with His own children.

But the entire feast is a spiritual setup for God's ultimate reveal: that God Himself chooses to dwell *in us*. We become the dwelling place. The next day after that feast is Shemini Atzeret where God promises to bless them in their work, their harvesting, and all their efforts to establish what He has given them. In Canada, this festival falls over harvest time and our actual Thanksgiving celebration and holiday. It's a holiday all about thankfulness and harvest, and an invitation for Father God to release continued, but new, blessings.

And here is the key: if the pilgrim has trusted in Yahweh as provider, and worked the land and planted the seed (in whichever way that applies to them since not all were farmers), God promises to turn their work into money and convert their labor into wealth so they can get whatever their soul desires. We learn of this amazing promise in Deuteronomy 14:24-26,

And if the way be too long for you, that you are unable to carry it, for the place which the Lord, your God, will choose to establish His Name therein, is too far from you, for the Lord, your God, will bless you

Then you shall turn it into money, and bind up the money in your hand, and you shall go to the place the Lord, your God, will choose.

And you shall turn that money into whatever your soul desires; cattle, sheep, new wine or old wine, or whatever your soul desires, and you shall eat there before the Lord, your God, and you shall rejoice, you and your household.

So literally in a few short weeks in the Jewish calendar, sons of the Father experience the feast of tabernacles (by dwelling in tents that represent temporary dwellings) and from there, God's children are established into the fuller reality of all the things God has planned for them. Which includes a physical shift from the temporary to the permanent. A home. A dwelling place.

This is echoed by King David in Psalm 37:4, *Delight* (from the Hebrew this word delight comes from the word 'Eden') *yourself in the Lord and he will give you the desires of your heart.*

I believe that we are now living in the timeline of these truths being made a reality in our own circumstances, being confirmed in the lives of the Father's sons. We can declare with our mouths what our need and desire is, and Yahweh will lead you us into a dwelling place. A place to know His presence and have rest, so that we are well equipped to go out and serve and rescue and deliver others.

Don't take this *only* to mean that you will come into possession of a physical dwelling (although that most certainly will happen for some). But it also means that many will find their rightful place, their home and community and tribe. The place where they fit as sons or daughters in a healthy and vibrant family. A home.

In the upside down kingdom of God, there are always new beginnings and renewal available. Bereshit is the name for the first book of the bible, that we translate to 'Genesis' in English. It's all about a new beginning. It's not only a new beginning but The Beginning of everything we know. It's when the sculpting of Adam and Eve took place in the garden. That earth shaking world changing moment where man became a living soul and took his first breath. Is there any more poignant a picture of a new beginning, than new life? The clearest example of this in our own day and age, besides birth, is the rebirth of salvation that transforms a person from death and decay into a new creation through Christ's eternal redemption and new life.

When we live according to the times of God and not the times of this age, as we establish ourselves in this restful Sabbath time of Bereshit or Genesis, we are determining in that restful posture how the *rest of our year* will go.

I am concerned that for some readers this will sound a little bit like a fortune cookie. And honestly in some ways, you could see it that way if you missed the most important part: when God is your Father you get the rights of Sonship and you will not have the same menial existence that many in this world will have! In fact a person operating under the spirit of this age, can not know the better ways of our Father in Heaven.

What I am saying is there are ways that God's kingdom works that are just so different than our worldly minds think. There is an actual calendar that God goes by, and it is entirely different than our calendar which simply charts January through December.

I live near a temperate rain forest and pretty much everyone living here knows that in March it rains. It rains and rains. In April we know that we will start to see beautiful purple flower bulbs blooming. In May we get an early Summer that continues warming through August when the heat waves break records. And so on. We know our own seasons.

Matthew 16:2, Jesus replied, *"When evening comes, you say, 'The weather will be fair, for the sky is red,' and in the morning, 'Today it will be stormy, for the sky is red and overcast.'* **You know how to interpret the appearance of the sky, but not the signs of the times."**

I am inviting you to enter God's timeline. I'm not going to share a card on the Hebrew calendar and get you to begin plotting everything out and get weird or formulaic about it. I'm just inviting you to get intimate and in relationship with your Heavenly Father so that He can reveal and point things out to you that you would have never seen, even if someone told you.

Listen to what God the Father is saying to you in this season. And even more importantly, respond to it!

In a battle between the Amorites and Joshua, the sun stood still so the Israelites could keep winning the battle while there was still enough daylight to ensure that their enemies would not be able to escape by cover of darkness.

The Father stopped time.

In the life of Hezekiah, the king of Israel pleaded with His Creator to show him a sign and show him that He had power to give Hezekiah more *time* by healing him from his terminal disease.

The Father turned back time.

The actual shadow of the sun went backwards, revealing that God your Father can even reverse time and turn back the shadows that befall you.

And best of all, the Word of God states, that the Lamb of God was slain before the creation of the world.

This tells us that God the Father is outside of time.

In other words, He's the Maker of Time, which means Time serves Him, reports to Him, and submits to Him. Time worships God, so don't become a slave to it. And it's in submission to Yahweh like everyone and everything else.

Let me encourage you with this nugget of truth from God the Father's heart to yours: the Heavenly Father is unbeatable because He knows the end from the beginning. And when you walk with Him, even Time is on your side.

A third benefit, powerfully revealed by Scripture, is that as a son, even death is a pathway to life.

When Jesus arrived "late" to visit his dear friends Mary, Martha and Lazarus, Martha had a gripping conversation with Jesus. Gripping would be putting it lightly, because it became one of the most famous and beloved Gospel-recorded conversations ever preached about, discussed and studied by millions. If what Jesus said in this passage is true, then all of eternity will be impacted by the monumental scene.

It was the Oscar winning scene (if you were to make it into a movie), where Jesus was setting up for the greatest miracle ever recorded in the history of human existence, up to that point in time. In fact, the only miracle greater would be the resurrection of Christ Himself!

First, let's read the beautiful conversation leading up to the big moment in John 11:17.

When Jesus arrived at Bethany, he was told that Lazarus had already been in his grave for four days. Bethany was only a few miles down the road from Jerusalem, and many of the people had come to console Martha and Mary in their loss.

When Martha got word that Jesus was coming, she went to meet him. But Mary stayed in the house. Martha said to Jesus, "Lord, if only you had been here, my brother would not have died. But even now I know that God will give you whatever you ask."

Jesus told her, "Your brother will rise again."

"Yes," Martha said, "he will rise when everyone else rises, at the last day."

Jesus told her, "I am the resurrection and the life. Anyone who believes in me will live, even after dying. Everyone who lives in me and believes in me will never ever die. Do you believe this, Martha?"

"Yes, Lord," she told him. "I have always believed you are the Messiah, the Son of God, the one who has come into the world from God."

Just take a moment to absorb the scene. The One who was slain before the creation of the world was standing with a woman who was mourning the painful loss of her recently deceased brother. Christ Jesus, embodied in flesh, was revealing to each of His future sons and daughters, what the power of death was going to look like when it came face to face with the One who triumphed over it. Through His timeless conversation with Martha, Jesus revealed that eternal resurrection was awaiting each and every one of His followers. From least to greatest.

The resurrection scene is not only about Lazarus.

It would be enough, if Martha were right, and Jesus showed her that in the coming kingdom she would be reunited with her brother. That would be the same hope any one of us, searching for hope, share after losing a loved one.

But there's more. Standing in the presence of death on earth at a graveside, Jesus was undaunted. Despite their attempts at stopping Him, noting the body of Lazarus had been lying there for four days. It was already decomposing and wreaked of the unforgiving smell of death. But knowing the power of His Father, Jesus the Son of the Father seized the earth-shaking moment.

But before He was able to change the game forever, Jesus gave us three more powerful teaching moments. They're directed at Mary and Martha in the story, but really, they are for us.

In verse 32 it continues, *When Mary arrived and saw Jesus, she fell at his feet and said, "Lord, if only you had been here, my brother would not have died."*

When Jesus saw her weeping and saw the other people wailing with her, a deep anger welled up within him, and he was deeply troubled. "Where have you laid him?" he asked them.

They told him, "Lord, come and see." Then Jesus wept. The people who were standing nearby said, "See how much he loved him!" But some said, "This man healed a blind man. Couldn't he have kept Lazarus from dying?" Jesus was still angry as he arrived at the tomb, a cave with a stone rolled across its entrance.

Have you considered this part of the story before? More often than not we stop to focus on the shortest recorded verse in the Bible, that Jesus wept. But it also records another emotional response. It must have been visible on His face, in His eyes, in His body language. Maybe in additional words that He spoke which were not recorded. Jesus was angry! It says it *twice* in the text. "He was angry," and then, "He was still angry." When you study the amplified version and other texts to garner the fullness of the original translation, you come to a powerful conclusion.

Jesus was not angry at Mary, or Martha, or even the mourners questioning whether He could have saved Lazarus from death to begin with. Jesus was ANGRY AT THE PAIN CAUSED BY DEATH.

Death was Jesus' final enemy. Death is our final enemy, too, because we know that each of us are appointed once to die (Hebrews 9:27).

So rather than just mourning and crying because of the grief, Jesus wept aloud because He was enraged at the pain and loss caused by death. He cried that bitter cry of agony, the one only those who have brushed up against death can fully understand.

Bitter tears borne of painful rage. Holy and righteous anger towards His final enemy. But, after an emotional time, maybe minutes later, maybe hours later, something more powerful than righteous anger stopped His tears.

The time had finally come. All roads led to this moment. Death itself was about to be turned upside down. Pausing with His eyes closed, inhaling a holy breath, with rapturous authority, He boldly gave the command:

"ROLL BACK THE STONE!"

Another pause. It was hard to tell if the next scream came from Lazarus, Martha, Mary or the crowd of mourners gathered by the tomb. At the Word of Christ, Lazarus' spirit returned to him. He came out like a mummified corpse in a horror movie. But, then the unmistakable, even more shocking moment arrived. Lazarus spoke. Lazurus recognized his sisters. Lazarus laughed at the beloved sight of His

Savior, Jesus the Son of the Living God. He was looking at his best friend. His brother.

And almost to the soul, everyone in that place was shaken. They just witnessed with their own eyes that Yahshua Messiach, the Messiah, Emmanuel was actually *with* them.

They had just borne witness to the most profound rule of sonship. For each son of God, even death will be swallowed up by life. It must be overcome. It is being overcome.

What looks like death in your life?

What smells like death in your life?

What part of your world, right now, needs the breath of God?

What have you buried behind the grave stones, calling the time of death, trying to protect your heart and move away from?

What is in need of resurrection in your life today?

Even the grave, death itself, can not hold you back from a revelation of new life and a new beginning, when you humble yourself and invite the Holy Spirit into that tomb. Sometimes things have to die for you to witness the power of resurrection.

Lazurus was dead four days. Jesus was dead three days.

Before the Holy Spirit entered the tomb, all the minions of hell thought they'd achieved victory over God the Father. But then, in a moment, an earth-shaking second, the blink of an eye by Father God, Jesus breathed in the Holy Spirit and death was finally and completely swallowed up in life!

As sons, we don't have to live the way the world lives. The Kingdom of our Father is upside down when compared with the kingdom of this world, and that's why if we enter fully into God's Kingdom, things begin to align the way they were created to be. When you start living like a son or daughter of the Father, you'll find that upside down is the new right side up.

Which is why we need not even fear death. Because it is the final pathway to life, and the life we will enter with our Father is everlasting, true life.

CHAPTER NINE

LOOK TO THE SON

When it comes to sonship, our ultimate source is the life of The Son, Jesus Christ. Knowing the Son steers the ship.

What fascinates me about the Son of God, was His determination to be known on earth as "Son of Man." The distinction between Son of God and Son of Man is paramount as we study sonship.

If Jesus wanted to, He had the right and authority as the Son of God to focus on servanthood or even force human beings into submission as slaves before their master. But Jesus never forced anything on anybody while he lived on earth. Jesus still will not force anything on anyone today.

However, Jesus does freely invite every son and daughter of man to look to Him, choose Him of their own free will, and learn from Him how to be pure, holy and humble of heart. He leaves a wide open invitation for us to learn how to be sons of the Father.

And so, the life of Jesus as Son of Man is our ultimate school in sonship. The power of Jesus as God, without Him embracing His humanity, would have minimized His triumph on earth. But as Son of Man, (despite being fully Divine as well), the "one man Jesus Christ" was also fully human inside a body of flesh, which enabled His triumph to be absolute, and greater than any other victory in human history.

As we study Jesus' life, let's remind ourselves that He did everything He did on earth as a man, tempted in every way, like we are. He overcame the pain, shame and insults hurled upon Him, AS A MAN, too. He was completely Divine, but His modus operandi on earth was to overcome the world as Son of Man.

Jesus refers to Himself as "Son of Man" eighty times in the four gospels. On top of this, the prophets called Him Son of Man about eighty additional times in the Old Testament. That's a label that He used repeatedly because He wanted us to learn about sonship as human beings. While our final estate will be Heavenly, in bodies that are resurrected and eternal, our journey into sonship takes place on the earthly plane. He never intended for sonship to only begin for us after death, after we enter the Heavenly realm. The Scripture's reveal that sonship is for every child of God, right here and now on Earth!

When it came to the question of whether He was "Son of God," Jesus deliberately let others call Him that, of their own free will. He did claim divinity in a few key passages, but ultimately, there was a profound reason for His choice to not call Himself "Son of God," but focus on the "Son of Man" label.

It is a requirement that every living soul decides for themselves WHO JESUS IS.

Let's look at three examples of individuals making their choice about the identity of Jesus in Scripture.

When Peter made his decision, Jesus made it clear that God the Father alone had revealed it to him. In Matthew 16 the disciples have a famous conversation with Jesus about His identity. He's being labeled by many, with varying conclusions about His origin. Some Jews seemed to believe in reincarnation, and said He was a re-embodied prophet Elijah, Jeremiah or John the Baptist (even though Jesus was already in active ministry when He was baptized by John a year or two earlier). Others believed He was some new breed of prophet. But in Matthew 16:15, Jesus turned the table. I would have loved to be there for this moment.

Jesus said, *"But what about you? Who do you say I am?"* Simon Peter answered, *"You are the Christ, the*

Son of the living God." Jesus replied, "Blessed are you, Simon son of Jonah, for this was not revealed to you by man, but by my Father in heaven.

When Jesus asked Martha what she believed in John 11, she was given a hint about who Jesus was, but made the bold statement of faith on her own about her belief that He was in fact the Messiah. *Jesus said to her, "I am the resurrection and the life. Whoever believes in Me will live, even though he dies. And everyone who lives and believes in Me will never die. Do you believe this?" "Yes, Lord," she answered, "I believe that You are the Christ, the Son of God, who was to come into the world."*

In Matthew 26, Jesus only ventured into the Son of God territory because He was placed under oath by the high priest and He could tell no lie. Even still, He was evasive about the title. *The high priest stood up and said to Him, "Do You offer no answer for what these men are testifying against You?" But Jesus kept silent. And the high priest said to Him, "I place You under oath by the living God, to tell us whether You are the Christ, the Son of God." Jesus said to him, "You have said it yourself. But I tell you, from now on you will see the Son of Man sitting at the right hand of power, and coming on the clouds of heaven."*

These Scriptures, and many more, remind us that we must all make the decision individually. There is no greater decision on earth for every living soul to make. Have you made your decision yet? Consider your answer today, and tomorrow, and for the rest of your life, because the revelation you'll find will never leave you the same.

He turns to each of us like He did more than two thousand years ago when He locked eyes with Peter, to ask us the very same question, 'But what about you? Who do *you* say that I AM?'

Peter, a disciple of Jesus and eventual apostle, made his decision. His life serves as a prime example of the journey from a slave of sin and this world, to a son of God in Heaven.

Peter followed Christ for three years, was among only three disciples that spent intimate time alone with Jesus, would deny his Savior three times, and later received a three fold reinstatement by the resurrected Messiah.

Three times ten years after Jesus was crucified, he was led away to a hill. Not the hill his Savior died on called Golgotha, but a hill of death nonetheless, traditionally known as the Hill of Vatican just outside Rome, to be executed. He would not deny his Savior this time, and they were willing to murder him for it. Displaying honour surpassing the greatest kings, he asked his executioners to crucify him upside down, because he did not consider himself worthy of dying the way his Rabbi and Savior died.

The life of Peter the apostle. A firecracker, spark plug and the flint-like rock on which Yahshua famously said, "I will build My Church." According to Catholic tradition, Peter was also the first Pope, but I prefer to call him the First Apostle, and the Church's First Pastor.

The life of Peter was incredible. If only his mother had known while she rocked him that he would walk on water, catch miraculous boat-sinking loads of fish and heal crippled beggars on the streets of Jerusalem with a touch. Not the touch of his hands or his prayers. He healed them when his shadow fell upon them as he walked by.

This was a man so overwhelmed by the Holy Spirit that when Nero, the antichrist spirit of his day, made up death lists featuring a long list of enemies of the state, Peter's name was at the top. He was dangerous in his devotion. He was threatening in His theology. A simple fisherman, history reveals, led the movement that ultimately overturned the greatest empire the world has ever known.

Peter became a true son of the Father. He was a true brother to the Father's Son when Jesus walked the earth. The rock that became the global Church built her foundation around Peter's faith in Christ, and his family of fellow believers in Jesus became the first living stones in the Church.

This rock would smash and somehow undermine the iron foundations of Rome.

Who was the apostle Peter before all these amazing stories? What made him tick before he walked on water, devoted himself to following Jesus or did miraculous works as a man of unique and bold faith?

As I considered and pondered the turning point in Peter's life, I heard a phrase that has resonated with me deeply ever since. The phrase was simple.

"Peter looked into Jesus' eyes."

And a question quickly followed, "Have you looked into Jesus' eyes lately?"

Peter did. And it changed his life. Peter did. And it pierced his soul. Peter looked into Jesus' eyes, and he wept bitterly. Peter looked into Jesus' eyes, and it made him the man he was called to be.

There are three profound stories of physical eye contact between Peter and Jesus recorded in Scripture that serve as an invitation to you and me to do what Peter dared to do: lock eyes with *your Messiah*. And do not look away. It's absolutely key to living and unlocking sonship in your life.

Peter comes off the pages of Scripture as a simple man. But without a doubt the Gospel writers are pointing out that he was willing to hold Jesus' gaze. Not only willing, Peter longed for that stare of blazing fire to pierce him, even when it hurt.

Few in the history of the world have known God the Father's goodness with the personal intimacy Peter experienced. He saw the King of the universe in the flesh, drew near to Him, studied His every move, every look, every miracle. Peter was there on the mountain when Jesus was transfigured. He saw his own mother-in-law miraculously healed in their family home, he witnessed numerous resurrections from the dead, he was disciplined by Jesus as a father disciplines his own beloved son. He also saw his greatest Love, his precious Rabbi, his true Savior, breathe His last breath on the hill of death called Golgotha.

The first time that Peter was arrested by the look in Jesus' eyes was the most important in many ways. If he had looked away then, he would have never followed the Rabbi. Perhaps we would have never known Peter's name.

So far as we know, Christ had not done any miracles at that point in His ministry. But there was a fire and a passion in His eyes that gripped Peter's heart.

Jesus was walking by the Sea of Galilee. He saw two brothers. They were Simon (his other name was Peter) and Andrew, his brother. They were putting a net into the sea for they were fishermen. Jesus said to them, "Follow Me. I will make you fish for men!" At once they left their nets and followed Him.

When he first locked eyes with Peter, it was the look of authority. In Israel, it was the pinnacle of Judaism to follow a leading Rabbi. But there was a catch. You had to be called. You had to be chosen. Peter was called by an up and coming, mysterious Rabbi, one the fishermen surely had heard rumours of, but would probably never meet. Yahshua. And when he looked into Peter's eyes, Peter left behind career, he left behind family, he left everything he knew in life, to follow Jesus.

It's dangerous to our comfort and personal vision to look Jesus in the eyes.

Peter and the rest of Jesus' followers looked into the eyes of Christ many times in the Gospels. There are other notable stories we could uncover. But there was a certain instance when Peter was undone by Jesus' gaze which is truly fascinating. It's a second time when Jesus pierced Peter's heart with just one look.

Luke 22:54-62 (ESV) *Then they seized him and led him away, bringing him into the high priest's house, and Peter was following at a distance. And when they had kindled a fire in the middle of the courtyard and sat down together, Peter sat down among them. Then a servant girl, seeing him as he sat in the light and looking closely at him, said, "This man also was with him." But he denied it, saying, "Woman, I do not know him." And a little later someone else saw him and said, "You also are one of them." But Peter said, "Man, I am not." And after an interval of about an hour still another insisted, saying, "Certainly this man also was with him, for he too is a Galilean."*

*But Peter said, "Man, I do not know what you are talking about." And immediately, while he was still speaking, the rooster crowed. And the Lord turned and **looked** at Peter. And Peter remembered the saying of the Lord, how he had said to him, "Before the rooster crows today, you will deny me three times." And he went out and wept bitterly.*

At the moment when Peter denied Jesus, quite incredibly, it tells us that Christ looked Peter right

in the eyes. He did so immediately after the third time Peter denied knowing Jesus.

Three represents completion or fullness in Scripture, so this threefold repetition signified an absolute denial of Christ. Peter, who left the safety of the boat to walk miraculously to the same Jesus whom he recognized just by hearing His voice, while unable to even see Him, that same Peter, denied *even knowing* His Savior and best friend.

In effect, in this passage, Peter was saying not only do I not know Him, I also want nothing to do with Him. Wow. After all Peter had seen and heard and done. Also, what a spear into Jesus' human heart. It must have hurt more than all the soldiers heavy blows to the head.

Yahshua, who knew all things, gazed into Peter's eyes. This time, when Peter looked Christ Jesus in the eyes, it pierced his embattled soul. Scripture tells us that he was overcome with grief, and wept bitterly.

There is a popular saying that many have heard, 'the eyes are the window to the soul.' It is worth noting that the Hebrew word for eye is the word ayin. It proves this saying in a powerful way. The Hebrew language fascinates me so much, and this word is definitely no exception.

It first appears in the Genesis narrative when Yahweh describes the tree of life and tree of knowledge to Adam and Eve. God the Father warns them not to eat of the tree of knowledge of good and evil. For by eating it, their ayin, their eyes, will be opened.

Clearly their eyes were open before that moment in the sense that they could see. Perhaps they actually saw much more clearly. They were connected to Yahweh. The Creator and His creation lived in true harmony. The spiritual and the physical plane were united. There was no sin, no separation, no shame!

But when they ate of that tree in disobedience, they woke. How true of today's culture! To be "woke" in our day and age means exactly what Genesis describes for us. The Father told His children the same thing in the garden: their disobedience would awaken them to sin and darkness and make them aware of both good and evil. But that knowledge actually separated them from their Father, it didn't bring them closer together. The rest of humanity's sons would remain prodigals to the bitter end without a redeemer. The rebellion was so tragic, so total, so absolute. There had to be a holy Son of the Father to make things right.

Jesus Christ was the antidote. He could bridge the gap and make humanity right with the Father again.

Their new state of wokeness placed humanity in the wrong battle ground. Although they, and by extension, we, may be able to perceive good and evil, the wakening to sin created spiritual blindness.

I've mentioned before that Hebrew is a colourful language where words are also accompanied by symbols or pictures. Even English letters bare striking resemblances to the original pictographic form of Hebrew. We get our English letter 'O' from the letter ayin. The Early and Middle Hebrew versions of the pictogram are virtually identical to the letter 'O' that we have in our English alphabet today. Put two beside each other, and you have a pair of human eyes. The English word 'look' makes even more sense now doesn't it? The word is a picture, even in modern English, of two eyes!

The word ayin itself in the pictographic and even lettered form, again meaning eye, or to know (think tree of knowledge), in the modern Hebrew form actually depicts a line from presumably the cortex of the Brain to two fixed points. The two points are indicative of human eyes. The Modern Hebrew version signifies that as the receiver of a visual signal, the eyes being that window letting in a signal or light source actually connect the image to the mind where the emotions and soul of the person reside.

This was true for Peter. He caught the gaze of Jesus and it pierced his soul. There are two forms of knowledge at work in the world. There is a knowledge of good and evil that does not lead to wisdom. And then there is a knowledge of the Kingdom that is all about wisdom and righteousness, and it leads to the fruit of the Spirit.

Sons of the Father are born for that knowledge. The book of Proverbs, which is a handbook for those walking in sonship, opens chapter one with a beautiful statement in verse 7: *The fear of the LORD (Yahweh) is the beginning of knowledge, but fools despise wisdom and instruction.*

When our eyes perceive the true Christ, our souls are pierced. We look into the true knowledge of the living God when we gaze upon Christ! And furthermore, when we truly see Christ, we also see the Father.

John 14:8-10, *Philip said to Him, "Lord, show us the Father, and that will be enough for us." Jesus replied, "Philip, I have been with you all this time, and still you do not know Me? Anyone who has seen Me has seen the Father. How can you say, 'Show us the Father'? Do you not believe that I am in the Father and the Father is in Me? The words I say to you, I do not speak on My own. Instead, it is the Father dwelling in Me, performing His works."*

So consider this! When Jesus looked over to Peter as the rooster crowed, it was as Peter's loving Father gazing upon His beloved, wayward

son. In Christ's eyes at that moment, bloodshot from the blows of the Roman soldiers fists, came a love so true, it shook Peter to his soon to be righteous soul. Therefore when you gaze upon Christ, you also, in awesome wonder, do gaze into the eyes of your Heavenly Father as well. That is the love of a Father to His son that places you in right relationship. That is the only source of love that enables you to walk in sonship.

As we'll see in the last story of Jesus gazing into Peter's eyes, the third time that they locked eyes was the most powerful. It was the first time that they both truly saw one another and became *one*.

The first instance of piercing eye contact, when Jesus called Peter to follow Him, was the look of **authority**.

The second look, at the moment the rooster crowed, was the look of **conviction**. A moment when Peter's flesh, his humanity, was exposed in all its ugliness. The conviction of knowing your sin and state of separation from holiness and life apart from a Savior.

Finally, Scripture records a third instance when Peter gazed into Jesus' eyes.

John 22:11-19, *Simon Peter went up and dragged the net to land, full of large fish, one hundred and fifty-three; and although there were so many, the net was not broken. Jesus said to them, "Come and eat breakfast." Yet none of the disciples dared ask Him, "Who are You?"—knowing that it was the Lord. Jesus then came and took the bread and gave it to them, and likewise the fish.*

This was now the third time Jesus showed Himself to His disciples after He was raised from the dead. So when they had eaten breakfast, Jesus said to Simon Peter, "Simon, son of Jonah, do you love Me more than these?"

He said to Him, "Yes, Lord; You know that I love You."

He said to him, "Feed My lambs."

He said to him again a second time, "Simon, son of Jonah, do you love Me?"

He said to Him, "Yes, Lord; You know that I love You."

He said to him, "Tend My sheep."

He said to him the third time, "Simon, son of Jonah, do you love Me?" Peter was grieved because He said to him the third time, "Do you love Me?"

And he said to Him, "Lord, You know all things; You know that I love You."

Jesus said to him, "Feed My sheep. Most assuredly, I say to you, when you were younger, you dressed yourself and walked where you wished; but when you are old, you will stretch out your hands, and another will dress you and carry you where you do not wish." This He spoke, signifying by what death he would glorify God. And when He had spoken this, He said to him, "Follow Me."

There it was again. With authority, "Follow Me."

When Jesus rose from the dead, note it was His third appearance to the disciples, there was an unforgettable moment of redemption, when Jesus restored Peter. Peter's emotions must have been swimming. The risen Christ was the same man Peter denied, just days earlier.

And painstakingly, but with tremendous love, Jesus made the point of performing a complete restoration of His brother and friend. Remember how many times Peter denied Jesus, and you'll recall the complete denial signified by his threefold rejection of Christ.

With a love difficult to fathom in its completeness, but bitterly painful in the buildup, Jesus used a threefold repetition to restore Peter back into ministry. The moment revealed a third way Jesus, and by extension the Father, looks into our eyes.

It's the look of compassion.

First, it was authority that drew him.

Second, it was omniscience that convicted him.

Finally, it was compassion that restored him.

Peter gazed into Jesus' eyes again, filled with unfathomable compassion and forgiveness and he chose, maybe for the first time, to truly follow Christ. It was an act of committed love, from Peter, that came with a devastating blow. If he chose to follow Christ for the rest of his life, his last breath would also come upon a mount of crucifixion.

What we don't often see is that almost all of the stories we have on record about Peter took place before he received the Holy Spirit. It was the power of the Holy Spirit that made Peter *brand new*.

We, likewise, need the Spirit to transform us. To make us new. Because even after all the glorious miracles and wonders he witnessed, Peter was nothing more than any of us would have been. A casual denier of the Creator and Savior of the universe.

But once he was restored and then filled and made new by Christ's Holy Spirit, he went from a feather blown by the wind, to a rock that Christ could effectively build upon. He became a solid rock that Christ would begin to establish the rest of His body on.

One thing we can credit Peter for, is that he looked into Jesus' eyes. More importantly, Peter didn't look away.

How many of us, catching Jesus' gaze when we've denied him, whether directly as Peter did or in passing ways, have looked away? If we have waned in our dedication to Christ, our delight in Him, wavered by choosing other fulfillments, have glanced away? Looked away from the eyes that knew us in the womb, eyes that pierce us with authority, omniscience and perfect love.

One thing I believe without any doubt is that Jesus knows you, and sees you clearer than you see yourself. If you want to look at Jesus, allow Him to truly see you. Let Him behold you gazing into His eyes with a desire to fully know Him.

Take pause right now. Close your eyes if you need to. Put the book away if you need to. Turn from the craziness of any grief or sin or purposelessness in your existence and commit an eternal act right now: LOOK TO THE SON.

It is intimate to look (and I mean really look) into someone's eyes. Some of us actually can't hold a gaze. There's something piercing about human eyes. They were made in God's image and they were designed to grip us.

Even human eyes can gaze with authority, seldom with omniscience, but often with wisdom or grace, and even love. Eyes can also cast judgment, doubt and fear when we don't purpose to regularly gaze upon Christ throughout our day, our week, or our life.

But when we choose to look at Jesus, it changes us. Peter was able to look into those eyes, and when he was restored, Peter followed with complete abandon. Even though promised that his commitment would ultimately result in his death, Peter followed.

And this is the kicker when it comes to sonship. When we behold Him, we become like Him. "You become what you behold."

In more ways than one, Peter became like Jesus. They both lived generously. They both worked miracles. They both died violently. They both sacrificed benevolently.

But while he walked to that mount of crucifixion, Peter saw the blind see.

He saw the lame walk.

He saw miracles.

He walked by crippled beggars and his shadow healed them while he passed by.

He saw the church explode like a grass fire in the heat of summer.

He saw lives transformed because he taught others to look into Jesus' eyes and not break His gaze.

He saw the Kingdom come.

He became a son of the Father.

In the book of Revelation, Peter's dear friend John saw the resurrected Jesus in a profound vision.

Revelation 19: 11-16, *I saw heaven standing open and there before me was a white horse, whose rider is called Faithful and True. With justice he judges and wages war.* ***His eyes are like blazing fire****, and on his head are many crowns. He has a name written on him that no one knows but he himself. He is dressed in a robe dipped in blood, and his name is the Word of God. The armies of heaven were following him, riding on white horses and dressed in fine linen, white and clean. Coming out of his mouth is a sharp sword with which to strike down the nations. "He will rule them with an iron scepter." He treads the winepress of the fury of the wrath of God Almighty. On his robe and on his thigh he has this name written: KING OF KINGS AND LORD OF LORDS.*

Look into those eyes. The fire of Jesus' eyes will burn up the garbage and fear and shame and doubt in you and make you brand new. It might hurt and surprise and undo you in the process. But no matter what happens, don't let anything break your gaze.

Look to the Son and do not look away. Blinded by pure love you will finally, truly, see.

CHAPTER TEN

BORN TO BE SONS AND DAUGHTERS

Son·ship - The right relationship of son to the Father.

Jesus was in right relationship with His Heavenly Father. Ultimately, the reason that He was able to be, was because He was 'in the Father,' and 'the Father was in Him.'

As we wrap up this study of Biblical sonship, it's important to reiterate that we must receive Salvation before the miracle of sonship becomes possible. But the moment that we receive Christ, we begin to grow into the revelation that we are not only part of God's family business, but we are part of His actual family.

There are so many stories in the Bible, but when you re-read them throughout your life, try to do something that I believe can enhance the message one hundred fold: read the stories in the context of sonship. You will find that sonship, right relationship with the Heavenly Father, is the quintessential message of God's Word.

Sonship marks the pages of every hero, every villain, and every nation in Scripture.

The heroes of the Bible (and by extension today), if we are being honest, are only heroes because they became sons. They inherit mercy and favor from their Heavenly Father, and the invisible hand of Grace makes their way straight. Think Abraham, Joseph, Jochebed and Moses, Gideon, Ruth, David, the Apostles and more.

The villains of the Bible (and by extension today), if we are being honest, are only villains because they refuse to receive the Gospel and become sons. They inherit hardship and judgment from their Heavenly Father, and this heavy burden makes their way crooked. Think Pharaoh, Ahab and Jezebel, Pilate and Herod, Judas, the Pharisees and more. They had every opportunity to return to their Father, but they not only rejected Him. They hated and refused Him.

The same goes for every nation of the Earth. If they submitted to the Father, they inherited blessing and glory. If they rejected His calls to repentance and spurned the invitation for Salvation, according to God the Father's justice, they had to be turned away.

And this is where sons come in. We take on the Father's business. The Father will stand firm to the end, offering grace, hope and Salvation. He offered His only Son, Yahshua, Jesus Christ. Now He continues to send His own sons, the brothers of Christ, all the men and women and children throughout history who said or continue to say, "Yes," to Christ.

As many as receive Him, He calls sons. Which is why I invite you to be transported, to enter the darkness of Barabbas' cell just moments before his release. But it's no longer Barabbas in the cell. It is you.

You are close enough to hear the hum of the growing crowd, which is being stirred into mob mentality madness. You strain to hear what you can through the bars of your cell. Rusty metal, a few tired soldiers, and that awful stench of unwashed prisoners the only barrier between you and your freedom.

You are aware of the chatter inside the prison. *One prisoner, in a prison holding billions of souls, will win the lottery and earn unmerited freedom.* Your name has been mentioned along with several other notorious prisoners. Leaning in for clues about what's going on in the courtyard, your fate takes a dramatic turn.

At this distance, you are stirred by the first shouts of the crowd. In troubling unison, you hear your own name with clarity that vibrates the bars of your rat-infested cell.

"_____!" (insert your name here).

Holding your breath, with goosebumps still rising on your calloused arms and neck, you hear the devastating cry that comes next.

"CRUCIFY them!"

The sensation of blood draining from your weak and hungry body. Pins and needles as the cry echoes a second time, "Crucify her! Crucify him!"

It has been decided. You have been sentenced. You crumple into a heap, hands weakly grasping the cold iron, defeated. A part of you always thought it would end like this.

No-one is more shocked than you at what happens next. The guards come for you, as expected. The hollow reverberation of your heavy, iron door pivoting. The scrape of metal on metal. Followed by a feeling that only a dead man walking can fully understand. Each step feeling like a countdown. You have only hours left to live. Every breath suddenly feels like a gift. It's the first time that you actually want to be locked inside your cell, maybe for a few more moments, if only to quiet yourself and have enough time to say a prayer.

But you have missed the rest of the conversation. Play back the tape from inside the courtyard. You

missed the first part of the miracle while you slumped in the darkness of whatever pain or trauma you've endured in your life. The part where Jesus, Son of the Father, takes your place. He's sentenced for your crimes, takes upon Himself your punishment. He is going to die in your place.

Like Barabbas before you, you believe, as you are hauled out of your cell, that you are the one sentenced to die. For indeed, from your vantage point, you only heard the fierce cries of the mob. Your name. And the sentence of death.

Oh the look in Jesus Messiah's eyes when you pass Him by! Envy and jealousy are not feelings Jesus Christ possesses. So when you catch the eyes of the true Messiah, you are gazing at the *essence* of pure love. Unbroken, unfettered, unrelenting, unbelievable love.

There are moments of significance in our lives where time just seems to slow down. Trauma can cause this sensation, but life-altering beauty can cause it too.

When there is a dramatic increase in a persons internal processes, actual events around that person can seem to take place in slow motion. I pray this is one of those moments for you. A

marker, a line in the sand, a reminder and a memorial.

I pray that as you read the final words of this book you realize that Barabbas and Jesus have the same name. And that is not a mistake or mistranslation, but is in fact the cornerstone of the faith of hundreds of millions of followers of Christ.

When you gaze into the eyes of Jesus, your name also changes to Barabbas. For the meaning of the name is "son of the Father." And if you've experienced the great exchange, like Barabbas did two thousand years ago, you share in that same, supernatural identity.

And once you become one of Jesus' brothers, you are in. You are part of the family business. You, my friend, become a son. So don't stop breathing. Go and share this message with the lost sons you know. Because our family, the family of God the Father, has a whole lot of room. Let's make sure every square inch of Heaven is full.

EPILOGUE

The blessings, the benefits and the invitation to sonship are the most incredible gifts that we receive after Salvation. The Son of God, Jesus Christ, provided Salvation so that we would become the firstborn of **many brothers.**

It's important to note that you will discover almost endless revelations about sonship as you read and study God's Word. I conclude with an invitation to you, to dig into the eternal and profound truths in the Bible, for yourself. Once you make a commitment to reading the Bible and studying it on a daily basis, you will find yourself naturally enabled to share the love and Gospel of Jesus with many. And you will not want to stop reading and studying, as the living, breathing Word of God brings you new life and joy.

I pray that God our Father will bless you and keep you as you commit yourself to Him.

Keep Breathing,

Daniel Kooman
July 11, 2023

ABOUT THE AUTHOR

Daniel Kooman is an award-winning film producer (*She Has A Name, Breath of Life*) and author whose work has been featured on The Huffington Post, the BBC, Newswire and ABC. His first book, *Breath of Life*, is now a 3-part TV Series directed by The Kooman Brothers, featuring *The Chosen* TV Series Creator Dallas Jenkins, Trevor McNevan of *Thousand Foot Krutch* (TFK), Kim Walker-Smith of *Jesus Culture Music*, the popular rock band *Skillet*, and Astronomer Dr. Hugh Ross from *Reasons to Believe*.

Daniel has traveled to more than thirty countries to tell stories that challenge and inspire. Story-telling has become a platform for Daniel and his wife Christy to invest in children, empowering orphans in Tanzania and restoring hope to young women trafficked in Thailand. Daniel and Christy live on Vancouver Island, Canada, with their two children.

MORE FROM DANIEL KOOMAN

Films:
Breath of Life Series (Writer/Director/Producer)
She Has A Name (Director/Producer)

UnveilTV.com or the **UnveilTV app** on iOS/Android

Books:
Breath of Life: Three Breaths that Shaped Humanity

Available wherever books are sold, or at **breathoflifemedia.com**

"Beautiful. The Kooman Brothers clearly have a voice, and it's an important voice that God's given them."

- Dallas Jenkins, Creator of The Chosen

NOTES: